WHERE AM I?

Also by A. G. Smith

WHAT TIME IS IT?

With Robert Livesay

DISCOVERING CANADA: THE VIKINGS
DISCOVERING CANADA: THE FUR TRADERS
DISCOVERING CANADA: NEW FRANCE

WHERE AM I?

The Story of Maps and Navigation

A.G. SMITH

Stoddart
Kids

Stoddart Publishing gratefully acknowledges the support
of the Canada Council and the Ontario Arts Council
in the development of writing and publishing in Canada.

Published in Canada in 1997 by Stoddart Kids,
a division of Stoddart Publishing Co. Limited
34 Lesmill Road
Toronto, Canada M3B 2T6
Tel (416) 445-3333 Fax (416) 445-5967
e-mail Customer.Service@ccmailgw.genpub.com

Published in the United States in 1997 by Stoddart Kids
85 River Rock Drive, Suite 202
Buffalo, New York 14207
Toll free 1-800-805-1083
e-mail gdsinc@genpub.com

Canadian Cataloguing in Publication Data

Smith, A.G. (Albert Gray), 1945–
Where am I?

ISBN 0-7737-5836-4

1. Geography – History.   2. Cartography – History.
3. Discoveries in geography.   I. Title.

G80.S55 1996   910'.9   C96-930809-4

Printed and bound in Canada

for Bert and Elena

CONTENTS

Where Am I? is the story of how people became aware of their physical place on the earth. In it, you will find out all about maps and charts — their invention, their uses, their development. You will also see how people learned to move about on the earth's lands and seas, and the tools they used to help them.

A few hundred years ago, most people were farmers. They rarely travelled more than a short distance from home.

Those who did venture further — usually fishermen, hunters or wandering herdsmen — had a keen instinctive knowledge of where they were and how to get back to where they started.

But as people started to travel more widely, they needed more than instinct to guide them. They began to observe nature very closely. They watched the migration of birds and fish. They paid attention to the direction in which the ocean and river currents flowed and the winds blew. Most importantly, perhaps, they observed the movement of the heavenly bodies — the sun, the moon and the stars.

It wasn't long before people began scratching the information they had gleaned onto pieces of birch-bark or clay. From these efforts, the science of mapmaking or *cartography* had its beginning.

It may surprise you to learn how advanced some early methods of mapping and navigation really were!

YUKAGHIR BIRCH-BARK MAPS

The Yukaghir people of Northern Siberia made maps on birch-bark. They left them at their campsites to inform other tribesmen of where they had gone.

This shows a trip made from a village on the Korkodon River (1) down the Kolyma River to the Russian village of VerkneKolmysk (4). The stick figures (5) show the hunter asking the Russian chief for a gun which he holds behind him. The hunter's route also took him by a hut on the Kolyma (2) and the village of a neighbouring tribe on the Yassachnaya River (3).

Birch-bark was also used by the Ojibway people of North America for making maps.

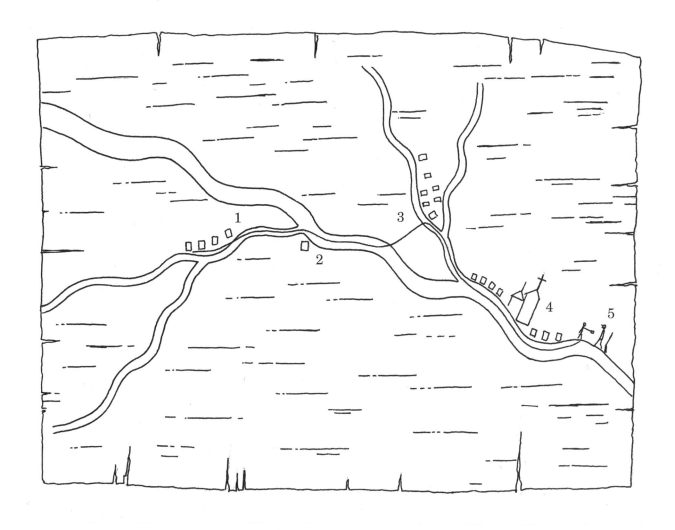

BABYLONIAN MAPS

Historians think the ancient Babylonians were among the world's first map-makers. They used clay tablets, writing on them with a wooden stylus, a writing instrument with one sharp end. The earliest of these maps dates from 2300 B.C.

Some were "real estate" maps which recorded the names of property owners. Others were city maps. In the late nineteenth century, *archaeologists* discovered a map of the entire city of Nippur on the Euphrates River. It showed the main temples, the central park, canals, moats and city walls. The Nippur map was from the period 1500 B.C.

THE WELL AT SYENE

In the second and third century B.C., Alexandria in Egypt was the most powerful and important city in the world. As well as huge palaces, busy shops and a bustling harbour, there was an elaborate temple to the Muses. Begun as a museum, it evolved into a great library and research centre.

Around 240 B.C., Eratosthenes was appointed chief librarian of the museum. A scholar of many disciplines, he had studied grammar, poetry, science, mathematics and philosophy. Erastothenes was also interested in geography.

Among the stories that travellers passing through Alexandria told was one about a deep well in Syene. This town was 5,000 stades (a stade is equal to about one-tenth of a mile) due south of Alexandria on the Nile. It was said that at noon on June 21, the longest day of the year, the sun shone directly above and was reflected in the bottom of this well. Also at noon on that day, no shadows were cast.

Eratosthenes believed the earth was a sphere, and this tale gave him an idea for an experiment. Ancient astronomers had observed that the sun was higher in the sky at certain times of the year and lower at others. It appeared to move between 24 degrees north of the equator and 24 degrees south. The lines marking these turning points for the sun were known as the tropics.

It seemed to Eratosthenes, from information he had gathered together, that Syene lay on the line of the northern tropic. This meant the sun was directly above Syene at noon every June 21. That's why it cast no shadows. (Shadows are cast by the sun hitting objects at an angle.) With this information he measured the earth.

How did he do it? At noon on June 21, he measured the angle of the sun at Alexandria. It was one-fiftieth of a 360 degree circle. Eratosthenes knew this meant that the 5,000 stades from Alexandria to Syene were equal to one-fiftieth of the earth's *circumference*. So the total circumference would be 50 x 5,000 or 250,000 stades or about 28,500 miles. The true circumference of the earth is about 25,000 miles. Eratosthenes' results were not at all bad.

Besides this achievement, Eratosthenes left an important lesson for future cartographers and navigators: if you want to find your place on earth, you must look to the sky.

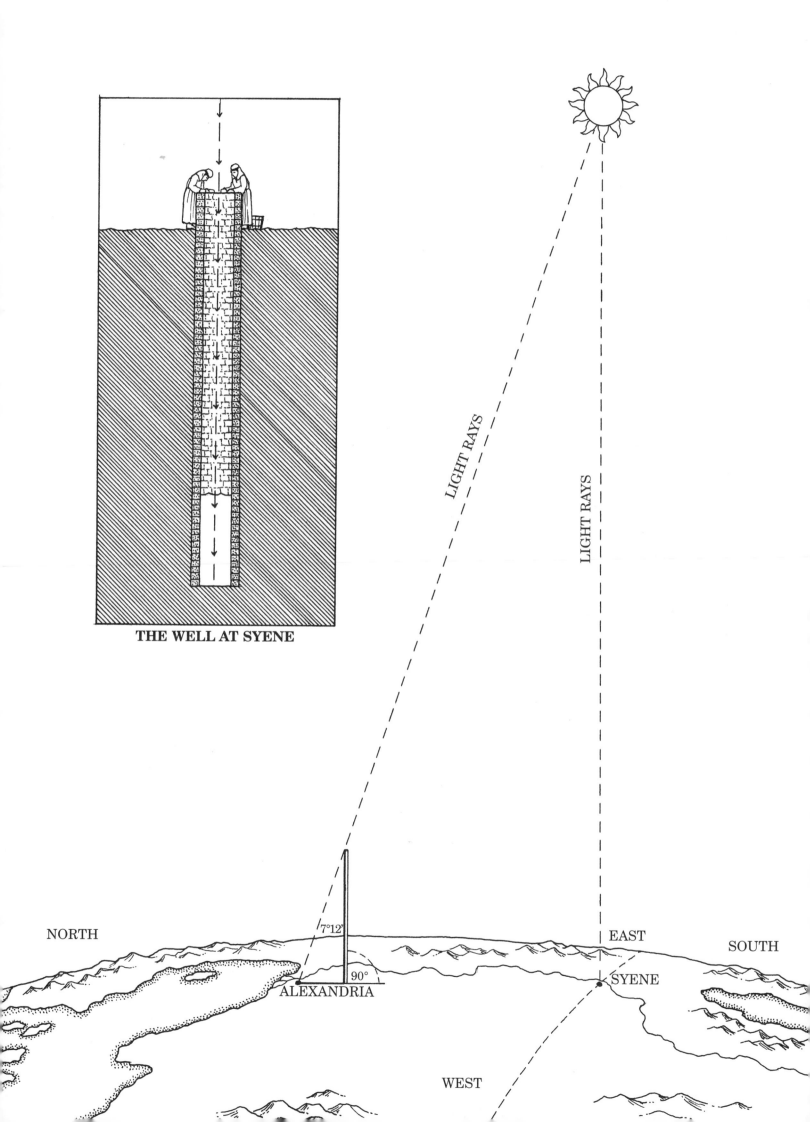

THE WELL AT SYENE

LIGHT RAYS

LIGHT RAYS

NORTH

7°12'

90°

ALEXANDRIA

EAST

SYENE

SOUTH

WEST

HIPPARCHUS' WORLD GRID

Hipparchus of Nicaea was considered the greatest of the ancient Greek *astronomers*. He worked in the second century B.C. He observed and catalogued over 1,000 stars. Hipparchus was also a mathematician and invented trigonometry — the science of measuring triangles.

Trigonometry formed the basis of Hipparchus' most lasting contribution to mapmaking. Using it, he gave us the 360 degree world grid. A grid is a network of lines which divides a map into parts. Today, different maps have different grids, but they usually give instructions on how to use them.

The Babylonians had divided the circle into 360 degrees based on what they believed to be the number of days in the year. Early astronomers then established the earth's three great east-west (equinoctial) lines — the equator, and the tropics of Cancer and Capricorn. Eratosthenes had drawn north-south lines through the great centre of Alexandria, as well as Syene, Troy and Byzantium.

Using this information, Hipparchus then established his own system. He based it on a series of equally spaced east-west lines parallel to the equator (the line that runs horizontally around the middle of the earth). He placed north-south lines at right angles to those running through the North and South Poles. Like Eratosthenes, he placed his *prime meridian* (the line which runs vertically around the middle of the earth) through Alexandria.

Although the instruments and equipment for mapping the world did not yet exist, Hipparchus had established a grid on which to work.

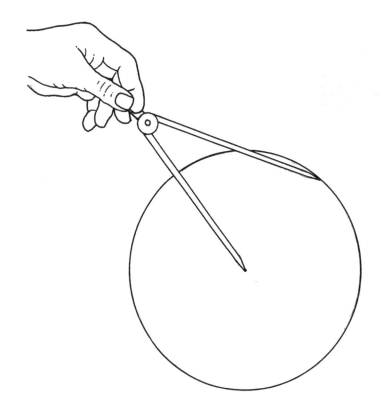

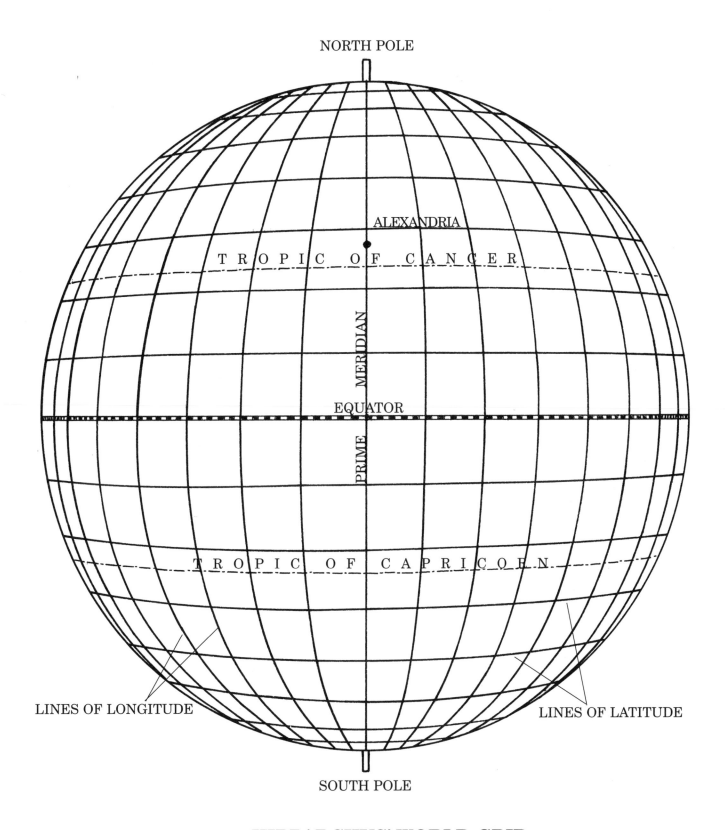

HIPPARCHUS' WORLD GRID

STRABO

Eratosthenes had defined the size and shape of the earth, and Hipparchus had drawn lines to divide it into parts. But scientists still didn't know much about its actual surface. They weren't sure how to position places they knew about — Greece, Italy, Egypt, Syria. And what if there were other, more distant, lands? Where on the globe should they go? Early mapmakers had great imaginations — they often invented lands to fill up a map's empty spaces!

In 25 B.C., Strabo, a young scholar from Pontius, came to Alexandria. He had studied with the best scholars in Greece and wished to study further in the Royal Library.

Strabo was most interested in geography and mapmaking. Using what he had read about foreign places and tales of travellers that he had heard, Strabo began to write his Geography.

Strabo believed that the *habitable* world stretched in a band around the northern half of the earth between the equator and the Arctic Circle. It went from Iberia (now known as Spain and Portugal) in the west to what we now call India in the east, and from the Island of Thebes in the north to the Cinnamon Land in the south. Between the different lands was water. But the lands Strabo named only accounted for one-third of the earth's circumference. What was there in the other two-thirds?

Some believed that, by sailing west across the ocean from Iberia parallel to the equator, one would reach India. Strabo thought there might be a second inhabited world that lay beyond the ocean. Fifteen hundred years later his idea was proven correct.

Strabo gave advice to future scholars about how the earth should be mapped. He maintained that the most realistic representation of the earth should be marked on a globe. He said that laying the world on a flat surface would be very difficult.

Strabo completed his Geography around 20 A.D. It contained all that was then known about geography and Western cartography. He had defined the problems. Now it was up to future scholars to try to solve them.

THE OBSERVATORY AT ALEXANDRIA

CLAUDIUS PTOLEMY

Claudius Ptolemy was born in Greece around 90 A.D. Like the other great scholars of the time, he came to Alexandria to study. Along with Strabo, Ptolemy laid the foundations for the study of cartography and geography. Ptolemy was also skilled in astronomy, optics and music.

Strabo's main interest in geography had been practical — how to place the world on a map. Ptolemy's approach was more scientific. He wanted to understand the entire world, not just the habitable part. He wanted to know how it related to the greater universe.

Like most of the scholars of the classical period, Ptolemy believed the world was a sphere, or globe-shaped. These are reasons he gave:

1. If the earth was flat, the rising and setting of the sun would take place at the same time all over the world.

2. The further we travel toward the North Pole, the more stars in the southern sky are hidden and new ones are seen.

3. Whenever we sail toward mountains, they appear to rise out of the sea. The reverse happens when we sail away from land.

By Ptolemy's time, geographers were already referring to the grid of lines that Hipparchus had drawn from the North to South Poles as lines of *longitude*. Those parallel to the equator, they called lines of *latitude*.

Like Hipparchus, Ptolemy divided the world into 360 degrees. He also divided each degree into sixty minutes and each minute into sixty seconds. He developed a system of chords for giving value to the minutes and seconds and projecting them onto a flat surface. This system would allow mapmakers to locate positions more precisely on the earth. It is the system we still use today.

Ptolemy knew that with proper measurements taken from the sun and stars, every place on earth could be located with accuracy. He described two tools he used for measuring angles.

The astrolabe or star measurer was used to sight the angle of the stars. It was made of a circle of brass or wood divided into degrees. A pivoting arm mounted in the centre, when pointed at a star, would give a reading in degrees on the circle. Ptolemy said the device should be mounted on a pedestal or tripod for levelling.

PTOLEMY'S ANGULAR SUNDIAL

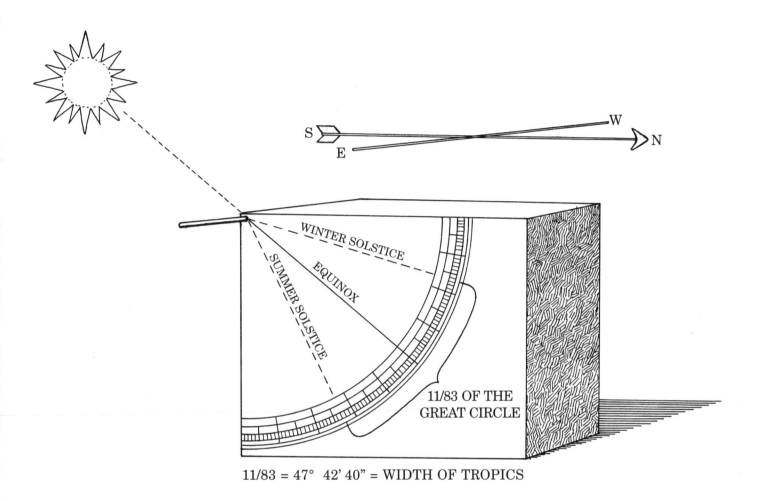

11/83 = 47° 42' 40" = WIDTH OF TROPICS

The second device described by Ptolemy was the angular sundial. This was a simple block of stone or wood with a gnomon (pillar or plate) projecting from the side. It was used to measure the height of the sun from day to day, rather than from hour to hour. If this device was placed in one location and marked every day for a year, it could determine the exact location of that place.

In the introduction to his great atlas *Geographia*, Ptolemy divides mapmaking into two kinds. *Chorography* deals with small areas such as villages, towns, farms, rivers and streets. *Geography* is more concerned with the larger features — mountain ranges, large lakes, large rivers and big cities. Maps such as these require the use of astronomy and mathematics to be drawn correctly.

PTOLEMY'S PROJECTION

Ptolemy knew that drawing the surface of a spherical earth on a flat map would mean a lot of pulling and stretching. So he developed a technique for projecting the globe onto a flat surface. This technique required great patience as well as the use of mathematics.

In his *Geographia*, Ptolemy mapped the entire known world on twenty-seven sheets. There were ten sheets for Europe, twelve sheets for Asia and

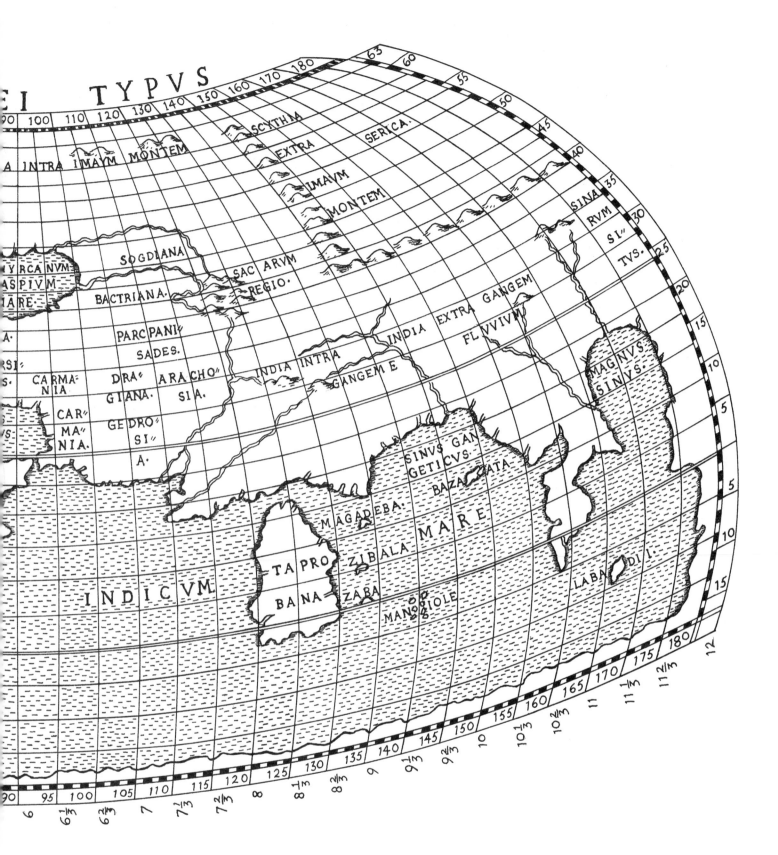

four for Africa. Ptolemy drew each map with north at the top so that people would not have to turn the book in order to read it. In the back of his book he made a list of places on the maps with their latitude and longitude. His work set a pattern for atlases that has lasted for almost 2,000 years.

Ptolemy laid the ground work for the scientific mapping of the world. It would, however, be a long time before his work was continued.

THE WORLD OF COSMAS INDICOPLEUSTES

Cosmas Indicopleustes, a monk from the sixth century A.D. produced the earliest surviving Christian maps. Cosmas began his career as a sailor and a trader, and travelled as far east as Ceylon. Later in his life he became a Christian and wrote on religious cosmography.

Cosmas believed that the earth was flat. He ridiculed the idea that people might live on the other side of a spherical world, as the classical writers had proposed. He said that it would be too hot to live there! According to him, all the survivors after the Great Flood had landed with Noah in "our part of the earth".

The idea of the Antipodes — or people inhabiting the other side of the earth — was impossible. "For if two men living on opposite sides placed the soles of their feet against each other's, whether they chose to stand on earth or water, on air or fire, or any kind of body, how could both of them be found standing upright?"

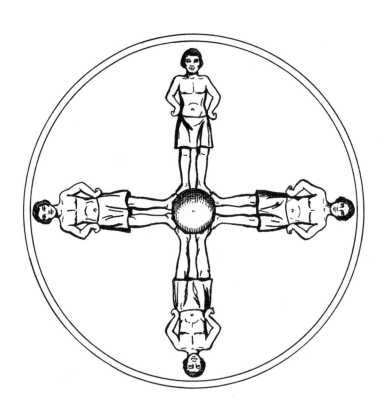

THE ANTIPODES

Cosmas based his concept of the heavens and the earth on a passage in the Bible. In this passage, St. Paul says that the Tabernacle of Moses, the tent in the wilderness, was the pattern of the whole world. Cosmas interpreted this to mean that the Tabernacle was a picture of the world.

He wrote that the world was a great tent with a rectangular base. The length was twice its width. It had an arched roof supported by four pillars. It was divided into three parts. The floor held the land and the sea with their earthly creatures. Above this, near the roof, hovered the angels and saints surrounded by the moon and the stars. At the very top was Christ with the most holy saints. To the north of the landmass of the earth was the great World Mountain behind which the sun went each night.

Cosmas' map was not scientific, but it was certainly very inventive!

IMAGINARY MAPS

Other early Christian writers believed that Paradise, the land of Eden, existed on the earth in the distant world beyond the ocean. Brendan, a sixth-century Irish monk, even launched an expedition to find it.

For five years, Brendan and his crew sailed about the western ocean in search of Paradise. Brendan came to an island and found a holy man there. He believed he had found the "land of saints". For over a thousand years after that, St. Brendan's Island was placed on maps.

Isidore of Seville, a theologian writing in the seventh century, was considered an authority on the subject of Paradise. In his *Etymotogies*, he fixed its location rather precisely. Using the Scriptures to support his view, he divided the earth into three parts — Asia, Europe and Africa. Each of these had been given to one of the sons of Noah — Shem, Japheth and Ham.

Isidore's map placed Asia on the upper east portion of the map. In the lower left half, across the Don River, he put Europe. Africa was across the Mediterranean from Europe and west of the Nile. Paradise was represented by a cross placed in the ocean far to the east of Asia.

The form of this map — a T within an O — was to become an accepted pattern for hundreds of years. Although other maps of this type were more elaborate — many were painted in bright colors and showed churches, castles, people and imaginary animals — the information they contained varied little.

Another convention followed by the medieval mapmakers was to place the Holy City of Jerusalem at the centre of the world.

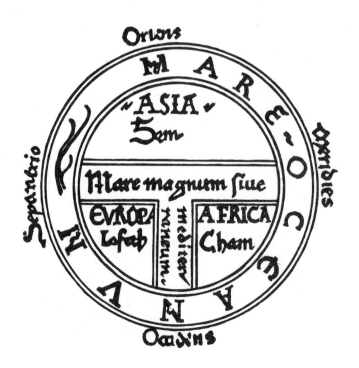

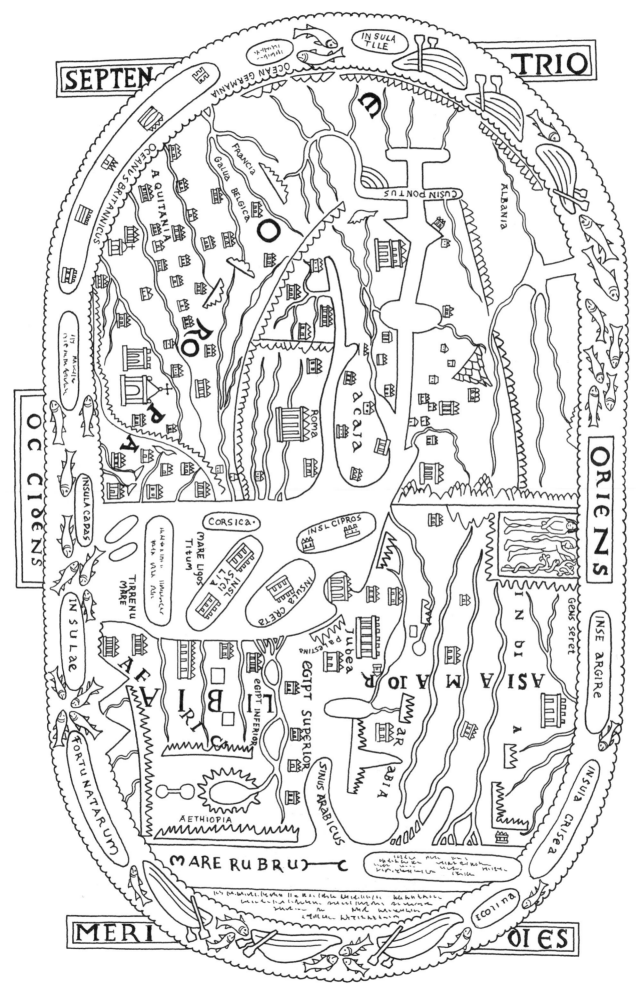

SEPTEN

TRIO

OCCIDENS

ORIENS

MERI

OIES

21

AL-IDRISI'S MAP OF THE WORLD

The collapse of the Roman Empire meant that many of the worlds' peoples could now occupy areas formerly ruled by Rome.

The Arabs moved out of the Arabian peninsula into the Middle East and Africa. They soon discovered the astronomical and mathematical works of Ptolemy and other classical scholars. In the ninth century they translated Ptolemy's *Mathematike Syntaxis* into Arabic. Under the translated title *Almagest*, it became known around the world.

Ptolemy's great *Geographia* was also preserved by the Arabs. They added their own knowledge of geography, especially of South and East Asia, to his work.

The best known of the Arab geographers in the west was Al-Idrisi. He had studied in Cordova and travelled extensively. In the mid-twelfth century, he came to the court of the Norman King of Sicily, Roger III. There he spent fifteen years compiling maps and writing commentaries on them. These were made into a seventy page atlas of the world.

Al-Idrisi also drew a circular general map of the world. This circular map was engraved on a large silver plate, which was later destroyed. Luckily, copies of the map had been made, and these survived. The shape of the landmass on Al-Idrisi's map clearly shows that he was aware of the work of Ptolemy.

AL-IDRISI'S SILVER MAP

THE DARK AGES

Following the collapse of the Roman Empire, the Western world entered a period of chaos. However, a new institution was rising — the Christian Church. This new religion was based on the vision of the world described in the Bible. Christian leaders viewed the writings of the classical scholars with suspicion. They forbade their followers to read these works. Holding views in conflict with the Holy Scriptures was heresy and a punishable offense. Because of this, mapmaking was to change dramatically in the next few years.

MAPS FOR CRUSADERS

From as early as the fourth century, Christian pilgrims from the west had been making journeys to Palestine. The Arabs conquered the Holy Land in 637. They were not hostile to the Christians, and continued to allow pilgrims access to the holy sites.

But then, in 1010, the Muslim ruler, Caliph Hakim, for some unknown reason, ordered the Church of the Holy Sepulchre in Jerusalem to be torn down. This act was considered an outrage by the Christians in the west. Soon after this, the Seljuk Turks who had converted to Islam began threatening Byzantium (now Istanbul), the Eastern Roman Empire. In 1096, the Byzantine emperor asked for help from the Christian rulers in Europe. The Crusades to free the Holy Lands from the infidels had begun.

During the crusades, people were on the move. Missionaries, merchants and armies travelled to the Middle East, and even as far as India. These travellers needed maps. Not maps full of imaginary places and mythological beasts, but practical guides that would help them find their way from one place to another.

They used strip maps and guidebooks — similar to those we obtain today before setting out on a long road trip. The routes were shown as straight lines from place to place. Castles, churches and walls were drawn to represent towns.

The Crusades lasted almost two hundred years. Many battles were fought, cities were taken and then lost again, thousands of people were killed. Ultimately, neither side really won or lost. The most important result of the Crusades was the reawakening of curiosity in the west about the rest of the world.

Wonderful tales were told by travellers about the wonders of the Orient. Stories of silks, spices and cities with streets paved with gold excited merchants and adventurers. The fleets of ships that had sailed from Genoa and Venice with armies of Crusaders now went out in search of riches from the east.

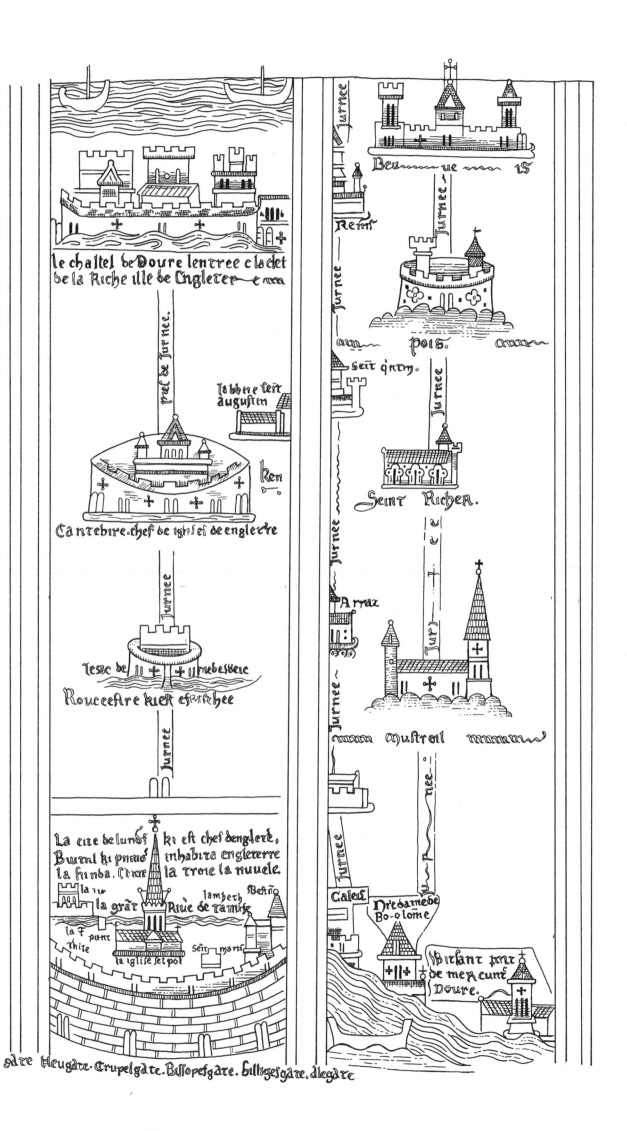

le chastel de Doure lentree clodet
de la Riche ille de Engleter — e

Prel de Jurnee.

la bbue seit
augustin

Ken.

Cantebire. chef de iglises de englecre

Jurnee

Teste de mebelsere

Rouceestre kiest esmthee

Jurnee

La cite de lundi ki est chef dengletre,
Buurnl ki pnmos inhabira engleterre
la hinda. Noms la troie la nuuele.

la tur
la grat   Riue de tamife

la F punt
thite   Sein marti
la iglise set pol

Beu———ue   15

Reni

Jurnee

Jurnee

pois.

seit qntin.

Jurnee

Seint Richer.

Arraz

Jur)

Jurnee

Jurnee

Mustroil

————nee——

Jurnee

Caleis   Nredamede
Bo-olome

Nrelant prt
de mer cune
Doure.

THE TRAVELS OF IBN BATTUTA

Christians were not the only pilgrims to the Holy Land. For orthodox Muslims, a visit to the holy Kaaba, a temple in Mecca, and the tomb of the Prophet Muhammad in Medina were journeys of great importance.

Ibn Battuta was born in Tangier, Morocco in 1304. As the son of a judge, he was well educated. At the age of twenty-one, he left the city of his birth on a pilgrimage to Mecca. This was the beginning of a journey that lasted twenty-six years!

Ibn Battuta's travels took him first across North Africa to Alexandria and Cairo. From there, he went by boat up the Nile to Aswan and across to the Red Sea. Returning to Cairo, he then set out north through Syria and down to Mecca and Medina in Arabia.

By this time, Ibn Battuta had become so taken with his travels that he decided to see as much of the world as he possibly could. He travelled next across Arabia to Basra and up the Euphrates as far as Diarbekr. After returning to Mecca to study, Ibn Battuta set out on a voyage to East Africa and travelled as far south as Mombasa and Kula.

By this time, he had acquired several wives, children and a retinue of servants. Ibn Battuta's voyages had now taken on the character of large expeditions. Wherever he went, he was well-received. After a trip through

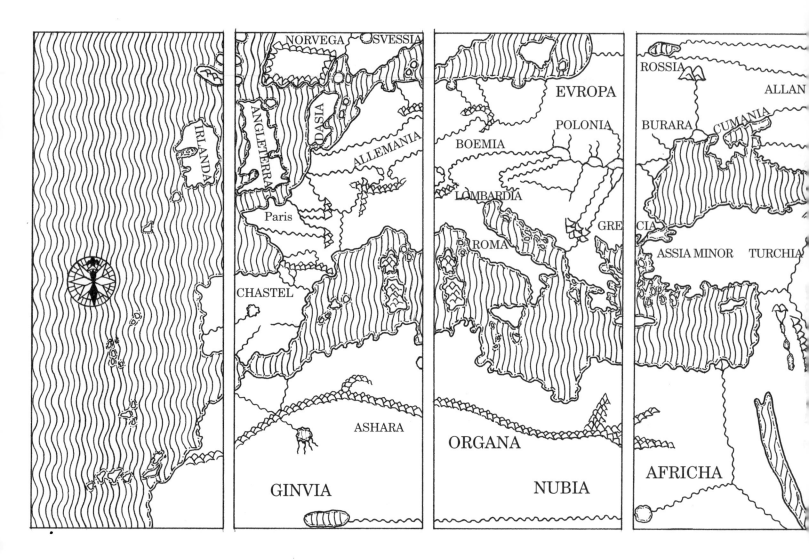

Turkey, the Caucasus and up the Volga River to Bulgar, he went south to
Samarkand and finally to Delhi in India. There the Sultan made him the
judge of Delhi — a position he held for nine years.

In 1342, the Sultan sent him as an ambassador to China. Although Ibn
Battuta had many setbacks, he successfully completed the voyage by way of
Ceylon and Sumatra. On his return from China, he made his way to North
Africa. In 1349, at the age of forty-five, he was back in Fez.

Ibn Battuta was still not ready to settle down. In 1350, he sailed to Spain
to visit Granada. In 1352, the Sultan sent him on a mission into the African
interior. Ibn Battuta visited the cities of Timbuktu and Gao on the Niger,
and brought his report back to the Sultan.

Throughout all of his travels, he had kept careful journals. The knowledge
he collected was a very important resource for mapmakers.

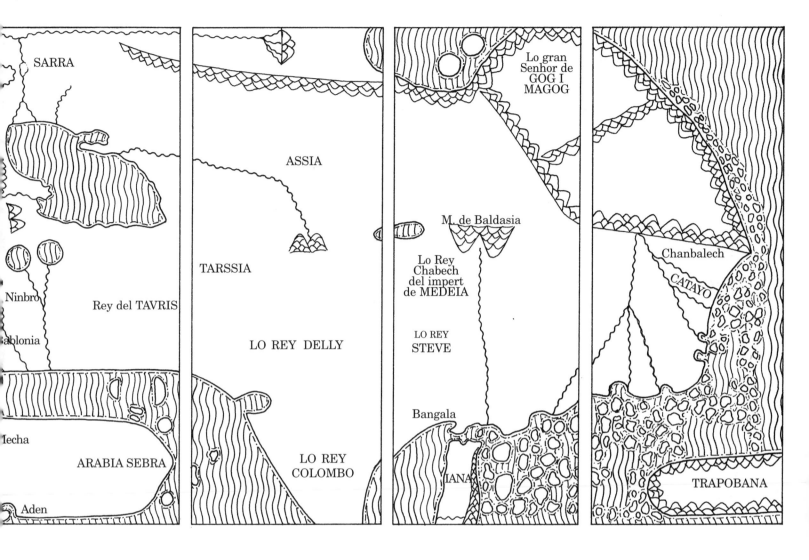

THE CATALAN ATLAS

Around the time of Ibn Battuta, even before the rediscovery of Ptolemy, atlases were being compiled, especially in Spain and Portugal. The information in them came from charts, observations by mariners and travellers' journals.

In 1375, Abraham Cresques, a Jewish map and instrument maker from Majorca, Spain, completed his *Catalan Atlas*. Although primitive by modern standards, it contained a wealth of information. Not the least important was the knowledge contributed by travellers such as Ibn Battuta and Marco Polo.

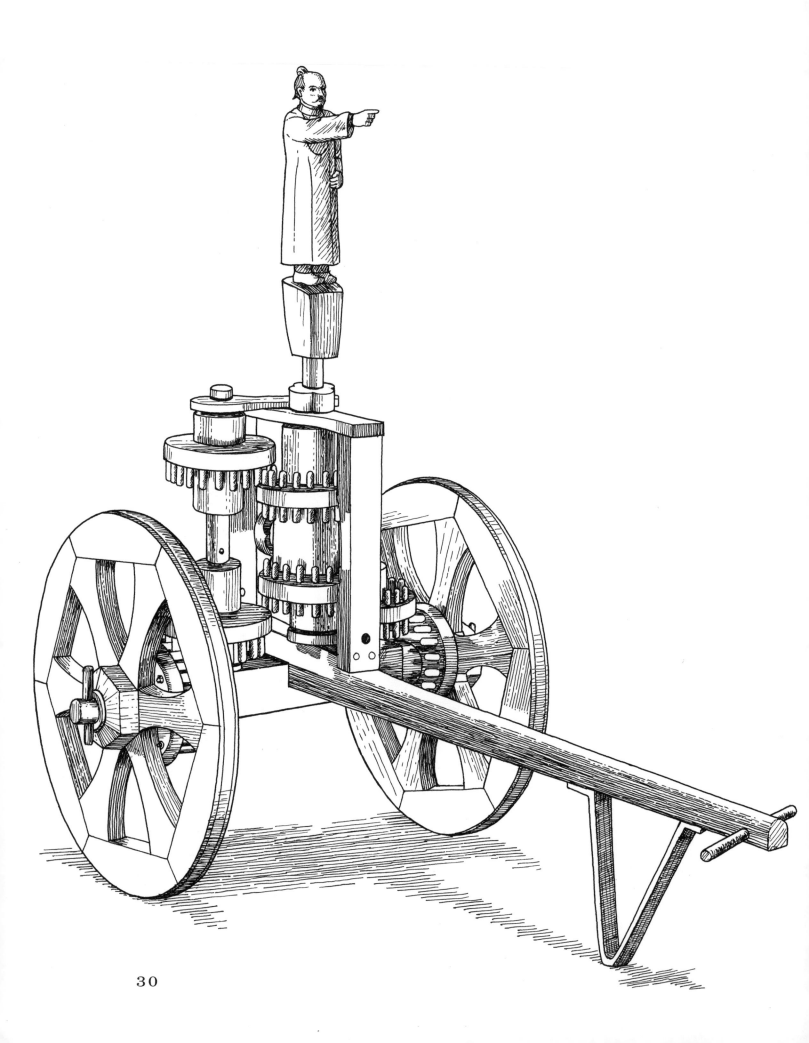

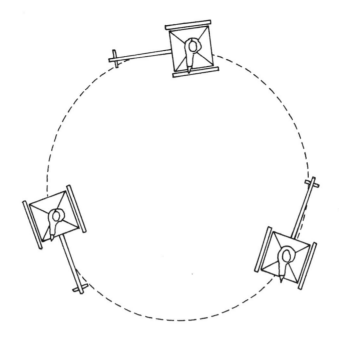

THE CHINESE SOUTH-POINTING CARRIAGE

Mapmaking developed in different ways, and often at different times, all over the world. For many years knowledge was not shared between countries, because they had little or no contact with one another. The Chinese in particular made great, independent contributions to cartography.

Scientific historians have wondered for a long time about the origins of the magnetic compass. In the late 1800's, literary and archaeological evidence was found describing a south-pointing carriage. This carriage was designed in China in the third century A.D., and functioned something like a compass.

The carriage had two wheels with a box set between them. On top of the box was a statue of a figure with a pointing arm. When the carriage was turned — in any direction — the figure would rotate on top of the box. The arm always kept pointing south!

Some scientists believed that the "magic box" contained a magnetic needle connected to the figure. Historians of technology now think it more likely that the box was equipped with a geared system similar to those in modern automobile transmissions. This mechanism would allow the figure to remain stationary as the carriage turned.

Although it was a fascinating device, the carriage was more entertaining than practical. On a rough caravan trail, the uneven ground would soon make the pointing figure lose its sense of direction! But the south-pointing carriage shows the early interest by Chinese scholars in the development of navigational devices.

EARLY CHINESE MAPS

There are references to maps in the earliest Chinese political records. The Rites of Chon (1120 -256 B.C.) required each feudal state to draw up maps and register its subjects.

China was united under an emperor in 221 B.C. Maps then became crucial, because the Chinese empire was so vast. When the emperor toured the country he travelled with a Royal Geographer whose job was to explain the local topography and products to him.

While the west was still in the state of turmoil known as the Dark Ages, Chinese scholars continued to make progress in mapmaking. By the second century A.D., a man named Chang Heng had developed a network of coordinates of the stars and the earth. In A.D. 267, Phei Hsui, the greatest of the Chinese cartographers, was appointed Minister of Works to the first emperor of the Chin dynasty. His great task was to make a map of the empire.

Chang Heng knew the map had to be drawn to scale. That is, everything on it had to be shrunk down by the same amount. This meant you could tell the relative sizes of one thing to another. The map would be laid out on a rectangular grid. The emperor wanted it to include rivers, mountains, cities and roads. Political divisions and boundaries were also to be marked. In order to make the map, people had to climb mountains and cross rivers.

The great map of China, when completed, filled eighteen sheets. It was drawn on silk, as were all the emperor's maps. Today, some historians believe that the woven silk itself may have been the origin of the Chinese flat grid system. Phei Hsui used the term "cheng" and "wei" for his coordinates on the grid. These are the same terms used by weavers for the warp and weft threads in textiles.

CHINESE COMPASS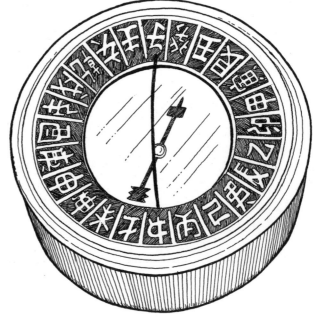

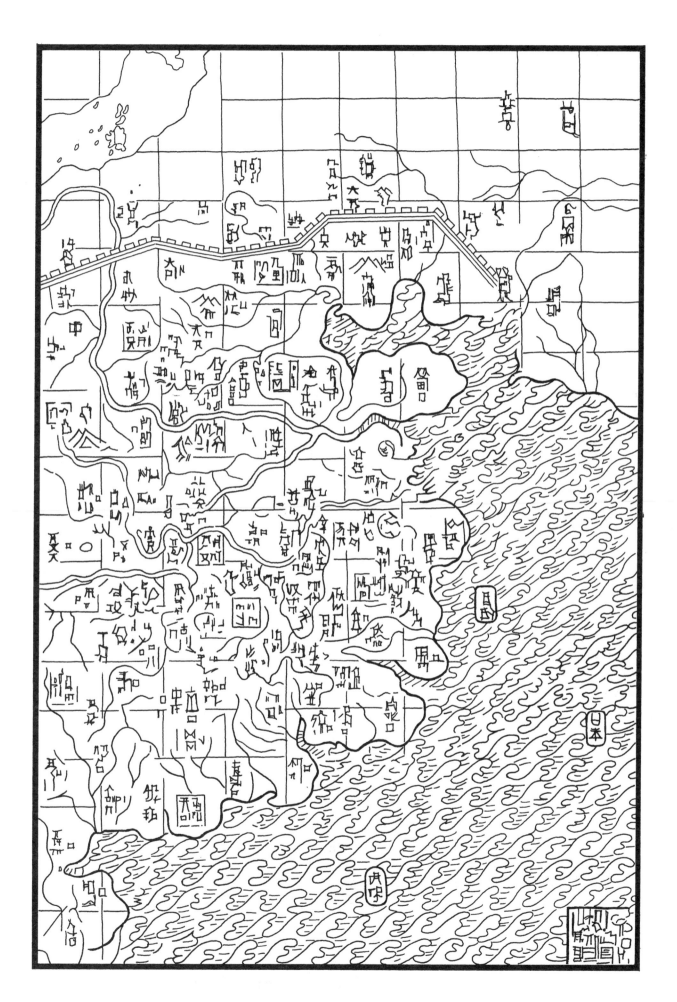

OTTAR'S VOYAGE

The Norsemen, or Vikings, of Scandinavia did not draw maps. Instead, they handed down the description of places they had been, and how to sail to them, in speeches and stories.

It happens that an account of one of the earliest voyages to the most northerly part of Europe has been passed on to us.

In the late ninth century, in England, a trader from Scandinavia landed on the shores of Wessex. He brought with him trade goods that included walrus ropes, ivory, and fine furs.

Alfred, then King of England, was an educated man. When he heard of Ottar's arrival, he asked that he be brought to him so that he might hear of his travels and have them recorded by his scribes. This is the story that Ottar told:

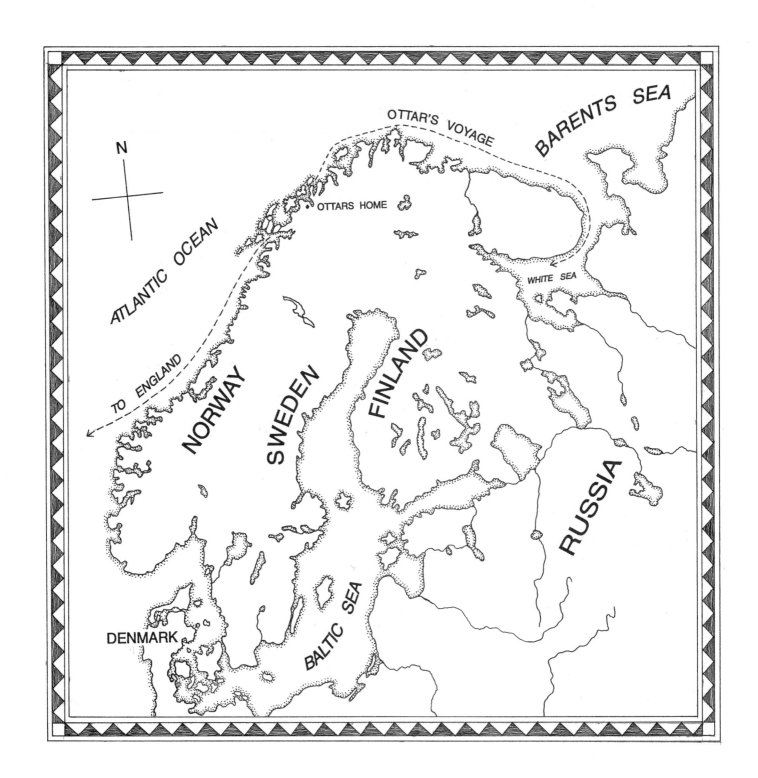

N

BARENTS SEA

OTTAR'S VOYAGE

OTTARS HOME

ATLANTIC OCEAN

WHITE SEA

NORWAY

SWEDEN

FINLAND

RUSSIA

TO ENGLAND

BALTIC SEA

DENMARK

Ottar told his lord, King Alfred,
that he lived the furthest north
of all Norwegians, on the Atlantic
coast. He also said that
the land extended very far north
beyond that point. Nobody lived
there, except for the few places
where the Finnas built their camps
for winter hunting and summer fishing.
Ottar told how he once wished to find
out how far the land extended due north,
and whether anyone lived there.

And so he set out along the coast,
keeping the uninhabited land to
starboard and the open sea to port
continuously for three days. He was
then as far north as the whale hunters
go at their furthest. He continued on
for three more days. Then the land
turned due east, or the sea penetrated
the land, he did not know which. He

VIKING SHIP'S WIND VANE

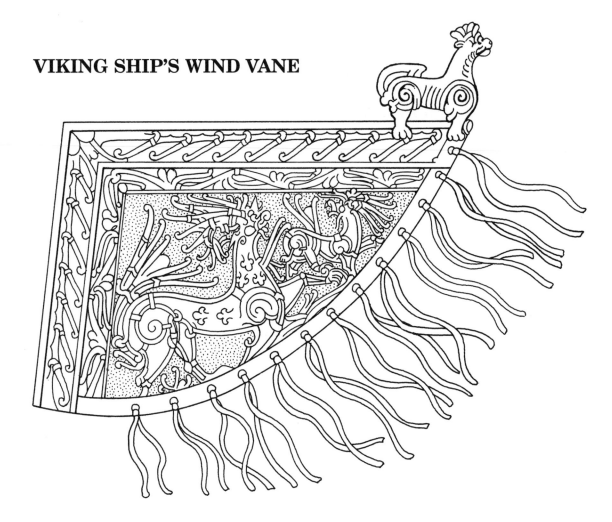

waited there for a west-north-west
wind, then sailed east along the coast
for four days.

Now the land turned due south, or the
sea penetrated the land, he did not
know which. Ottar waited for a due
northern wind. Then he sailed due
south along the coast for five days.
A great river went up into the land
there.

Ottar and his men sailed into the
river. They did not dare sail
beyond it, because they knew the
land on the river's far side was
fully settled ...

The Norsemen continued their explorations in the north Atlantic. They
settled the Faroe Islands and Iceland, and established colonies in Greenland.

Around the year 1000, the Norsemen reached the shores of North America.
They did not stay. They found the continent inhabited by native people, and
were unable to establish a permanent settlement there.

THE EARLY NAVIGATORS

Seafarers of the early Mediterranean cultures, the Greeks and Phoenicians, had long understood the movement of the stars and how to sail by them. The Phoenicians had books that gave sailing directions based on astronomical observation. The books also contained information about where to find fresh water and firewood.

Before the compass was invented, mariners needed a way to describe direction. For this purpose, they developed the wind rose. This was a card divided into quarters based on the rising sun (the east), the setting sun (the west), the darkness (the north, or the bear) and the light (the south, or opposite the bear).

Some historians of navigation believe that the Vikings developed a solar compass. Recent archaeological discoveries in the Norse settlements of Greenland bear this out. Tests of modern solar compasses have found them to be surprisingly accurate.

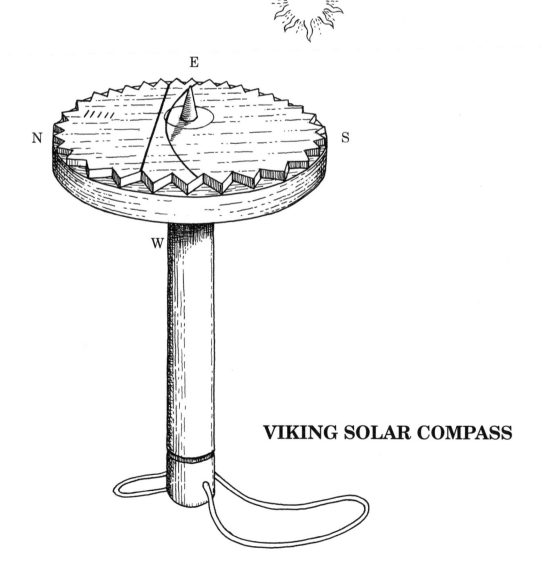

VIKING SOLAR COMPASS

THE MAGNETIC COMPASS

The magnetic *compass* is considered the greatest of all inventions for finding one's direction.

As early as the fourth century, writers such as St. Augustine had described a magical kind of iron ore — magnetite. When a needle was rubbed with this magnetite or loadstone, and mounted so that it could swing freely, it would always point in a north/south direction.

The properties of the loadstone were known in China. In fact, some of the best specimens came from there, as well as Bengal and the East Indies. Some were so strong they could lift their own weight in iron!

The earliest mariner's compasses were simply corks or straws floated in a dish of water, with magnetized needles pushed through them. Eventually, sailors came up with the idea of attaching the magnetized needle to the wind rose. They then mounted the whole apparatus on a pivot that allowed it to swing freely.

The mariner's compass that we know today has changed little in the seven or eight hundred years since it was invented. Now, most compasses are suspended in alcohol — to prevent freezing — and mounted in boxes that can swing in any direction.

Around 1450 to 1500, sailors began to notice that their compasses did not always point to the North Star. They didn't know why, but they adjusted them to account for the few degrees of local variation. It was not until much later that it was discovered that the *Magnetic North Pole* and True North Pole were not in the same location. Today, most nautical charts give the local compass variation from True North.

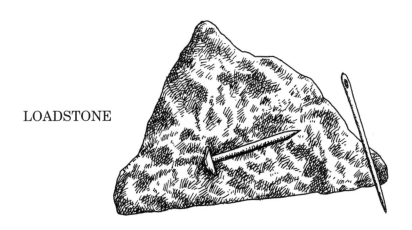

LOADSTONE

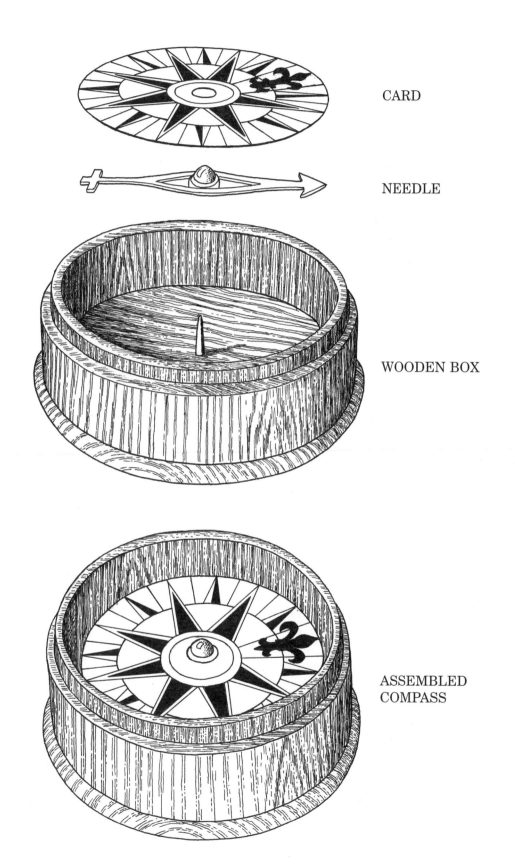

CARD

NEEDLE

WOODEN BOX

ASSEMBLED
COMPASS

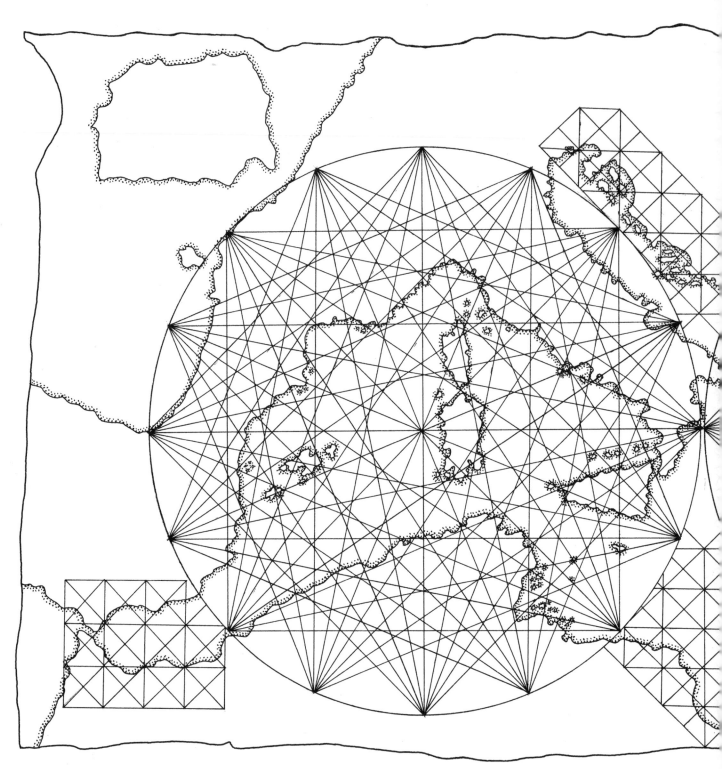

EARLY CHARTS AND TABLES

For centuries, sea captains had been compiling sailing directions. These were written descriptions of things to look for when sailing from one port to another. They included hazards along the way, how to enter harbours, and, often, crude charts.

With the invention of the compass, the mariners were able to give directions more exactly. The earliest charts to include compass directions were drawn by Italian navigators in the fourteenth century. They were called

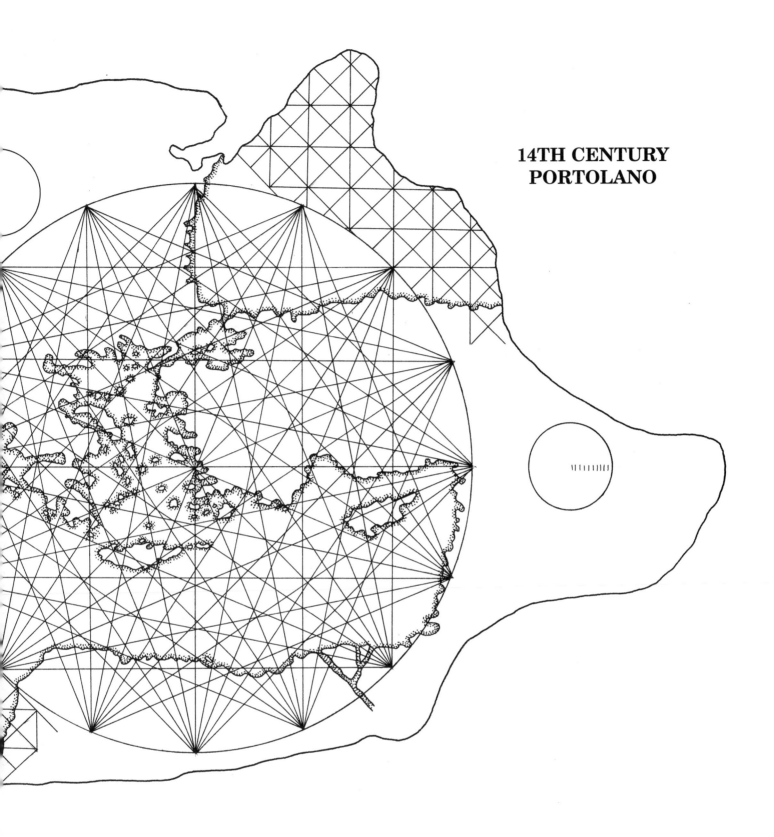

"portolanos". They were not based on a grid system but on compass courses and estimated distances. Coastal outlines on these early charts are quite accurate.

Early sea charts were closely guarded secrets. They were often weighted so that they could be thrown overboard and sunk in the event of capture by enemy ships or pirates. Accurate charts were very valuable. They gave a sea captain an edge over his rivals and seafaring nations an advantage over their enemies.

THE PORTUGUESE NAVIGATORS

In the twelfth and thirteenth centuries, new kingdoms were emerging on the Iberian peninsula. The kingdoms of Castile, Leon, Aragon and Portugal were now all rivals for power on the peninsula.

Portugal's strength was its ability as a seafaring nation. King Diniz issued laws encouraging trade and commerce overseas. He encouraged Genoese seamen to come to Portugal. Ferdinand I succeeded him and continued to promote shipbuilding and trade. By the end of the fourteenth century, Lisbon had become an international port and the Madeira and Canary Islands had been discovered.

In 1415, the Muslim city of Ceuta was captured by the Portuguese, led by the young Prince Henry. Ceuta was strategically very important and gave Portugal a foothold on the African continent.

Caravans had long travelled across the "sea of sand" from Tunisia to Timbuktu. The trip was said to take thirty-seven days. Beyond Timbuktu lay Ghana and the Gold Coast of Africa. Prince Henry, who was only twenty-one years old when Ceuta fell, wanted to gain the riches of Africa for Portugal. But the interior of Africa was firmly in the control of the Moors.

Henry turned his attention to the sea. He began outfitting ships for expeditions along the coast of Africa. In 1432, the Azores were discovered and soon colonized. Encouraged by this success, Henry founded a nautical academy at Sagres and a shipyard at Lagos.

Jafuda Cresques was hired to train pilots and cartographers. He made navigation instruments — astrolabes, quadrants and compasses — for the mariners. The navigators were taught how to find their latitude by measuring the angle between the North Star, Polaris and the horizon.

The Portuguese expeditions continued down the coast of Africa. In 1445, the explorer Nuno Tristao reached Senegal. While little gold was found, slaves were captured and sold, making the expeditions a profitable venture.

In 1447, Juan Fernandez had himself set ashore at Rio d'Ouro. He wanted to know more about the land and people of West Africa — the Azenegs, the Berbers and the Arabs. He had learned the Azenegs' language from a slave in Portugal, and travelled into the interior with Azeneg guides.

All of the information gathered by the Portuguese explorers was brought back to Prince Henry — now called "The Navigator" — in Portugal. At the academy in Sagres, it was incorporated into charts, and new expeditions were launched.

THE SCIENCE OF LATITUDE

Determining one's latitude is important to navigators. To do this, two pieces of information are needed: the angle of elevation of the sun or a particular star above the horizon; and the position of that particular celestial body on any given day of the year.

Astronomers had been collecting information about the movement and position of stars for several thousand years. They also plotted the track of the sun across the sky and the *precession of the equinoxes*. They compiled this information into tables, or almanacs. The geographical postion of a particular star at a particular time could be found by referring to these tables. They give the precise position of the heavenly bodies at frequent intervals each day and night.

The earliest *almanacs* included astrological symbols and other information that was of no use to mapmakers and navigators. In 1509, a small pamphlet of twenty-four pages was published in Portugal. It included data on the position of the sun and the Pole Star, as well as instructions on how to calculate one's latitude. There was also a list of the latitudes of known places. Of special interest to seamen was a method for calculating the distance traversed by a ship over its course. This was practical information that navigators could use.

Although latitude and longitude are now thought of together, it was actually several centuries after latitude was mastered that the science of longitude was developed.

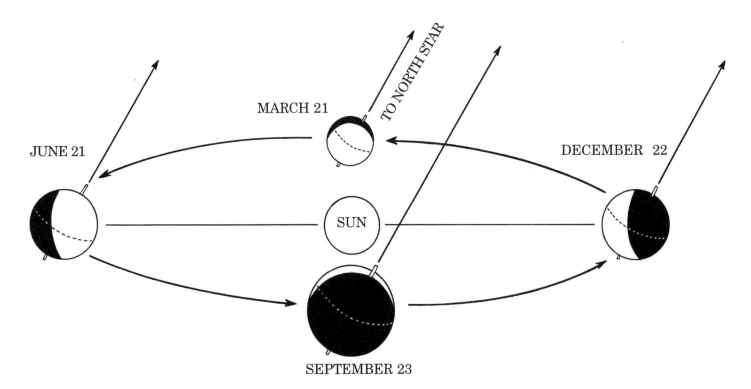

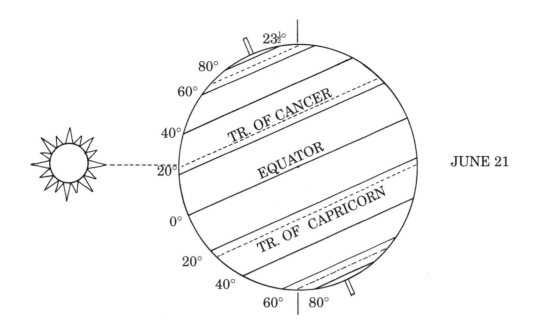

JUNE 21

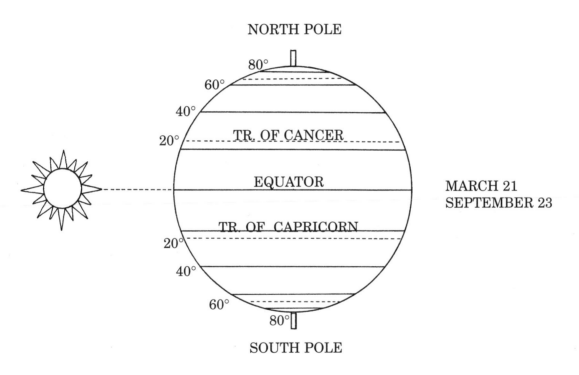

NORTH POLE

MARCH 21
SEPTEMBER 23

SOUTH POLE

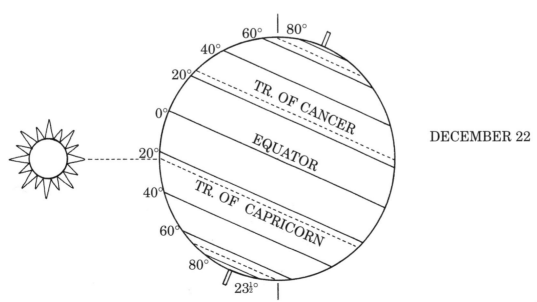

DECEMBER 22

EARLY INSTRUMENTS

Scholars and seafarers now understood that if accurate measurements of the positions of the heavenly bodies could be taken at sea, sailors could know their latitude with some certainty. What was needed were adequate instruments to do the job.

Astrolabes, or "star measurers" had been described by Ptolemy. Large ones were used by astronomers in observatories. Small ones were made for use on ships. It took three men — one to hold the thumb ring; one to take the sight; and one to read the dial — to get a reading. And the readings were not very accurate when taken from the deck of a rolling ship! Whenever possible, navigators landed to take their sightings.

The cross-staff was used by ancient astronomers for measuring the latitude of stars. It was adopted by seamen for use at sea. The instrument consisted of a staff and a cross piece. The lower end of the cross was positioned on the horizon. Sighting along the staff, the cross was slid until it touched the object (the sun or a star) being observed. The reading was taken from marks indicating degrees along the staff. Only one person was needed to use it.

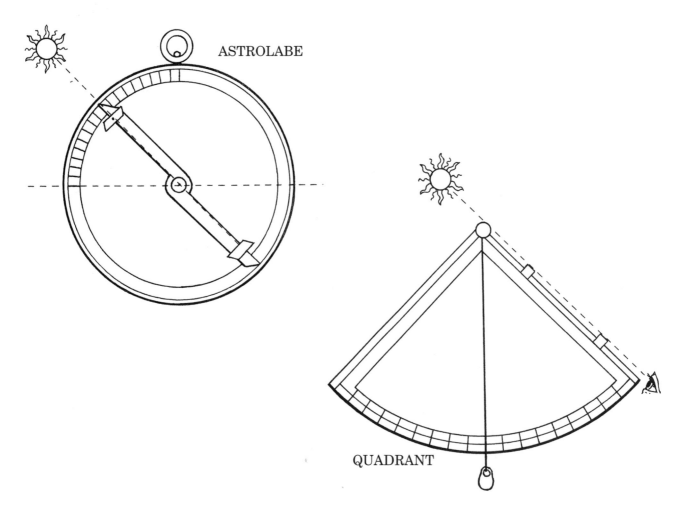

ASTROLABE

QUADRANT

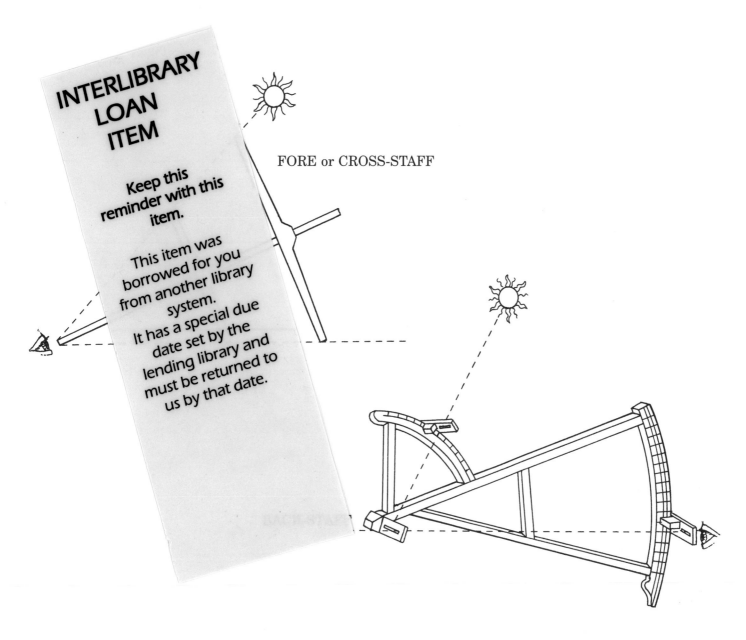

FORE or CROSS-STAFF

Both the astrolabe and cross-staff required that the observer look directly into the sun. On bright days, the glare was blinding. To solve this problem, the English sea captain and navigator John Davis invented the back-staff. It consisted of a staff with a sliding half-cross or transom. The observer began by turning his back to the sun. Then he slid the transom along the staff until it cast a shadow on a small plate at the front. Through this, the observer could sight the horizon.

John Davis also invented the quadrant, with the help of Edward Wright, a mathematician from Cambridge. This device had an eye piece on a transom through which the observer sighted the horizon and the reflected sun.

Pierre Bouguer, a professor of *hydrography* at Croissic, made further improvements to the quadrant, including a transom to bring down the reflected sun to the horizon.

The octant was developed in England by John Hadley and first tested in 1732. It included a reflecting telescope and spirit level, and was much more accurate than any other instrument previously used at sea.

TRAVERSE BOARDS

By 1600 navigators were using traverse boards for reckoning the position of a ship on its course. At the top of the board was a compass rose with eight holes for pegs drilled in each of the thirty-two points. Pegs were hung from cords in the centre. Each half hour, as the ship sailed along its course, the helmsman on watch would place a peg in the point of sail — north, north-east, east, etc. — travelled. Time was kept with a sand glass.

The rows of holes along the bottom of the board were for calculating the speed of the ship in nautical miles or knots and tenths of a knot. Once each

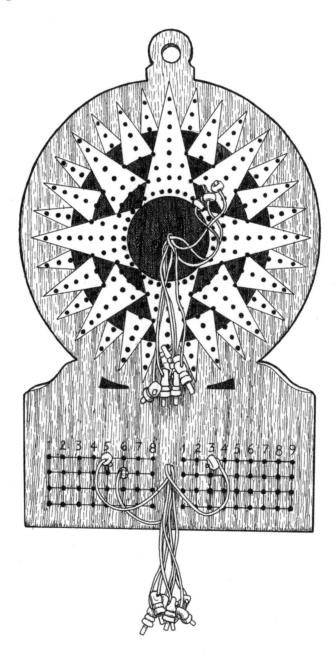

hour the speed was checked using a log and line. The log consisted of a small weighted board or "chip" thrown over the side of the ship to which was tied a line. The line, knotted at set intervals, rolled off a reel as the navigator watched a small sand glass. (This was usually a thirty second glass.) When the sand ran out of the glass, the cord was brought in and the number of knots that had passed over the side was recorded. At the end of a four-hour watch, the navigator or captain entered the information from the traverse board in the ship's log book and calculated the position of the ship.

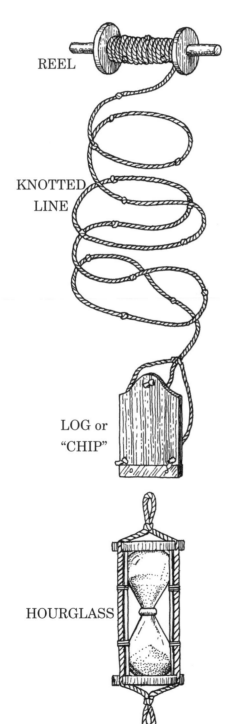

REEL

KNOTTED LINE

LOG or "CHIP"

HOURGLASS

HOUR	KNOTS	1/10'S	COURSE
2	3	2	North by Northeast
4	2	4	North by Northeast
6	4	2	Northeast
8	5	3	Northeast
10	2	3 $\frac{1}{4}$	North by Northeast
12	3	5	North by Northeast
2	2	3	Northeast by East
4	2	4	Northeast
6	6	1	North
8	6	3	Northeast by North
10	6	2	North by Northeast
12	3	4	North by Northeast

PAGE OF SHIP'S LOG

SOUNDINGS

Soundings are taken to learn the depth of water and to determine the condition of the bottom. The sounding lead and line are one of the most ancient tools of the navigator and chartmaker. Although different types of weights and lengths of line were used over the centuries, their purpose was the same.

The length of line attached to the common hand lead is divided into fathoms (1 fathom = 6 feet). On it, the depth is marked with strips of leather or cloth tied at each fathom — two strips for two fathoms, three strips for three fathoms, one white cloth for five fathoms, etc.

At the end of the line is tied the sounding lead. The deep-sea lead is usually sixteen to twenty pounds. The bottom end is hollow. Tallow or grease is put in the hollow so that mud, sand or gravel on the bottom will stick to it, and a sample may be taken.

The condition of the bottom is important to sailors anchoring their ships. Fishermen can learn from the bottom conditions what fish might be feeding there. On modern navigational charts, the depths are marked in fathoms and feet. The conditions of the bottom are also marked — M for mud, R for rock.

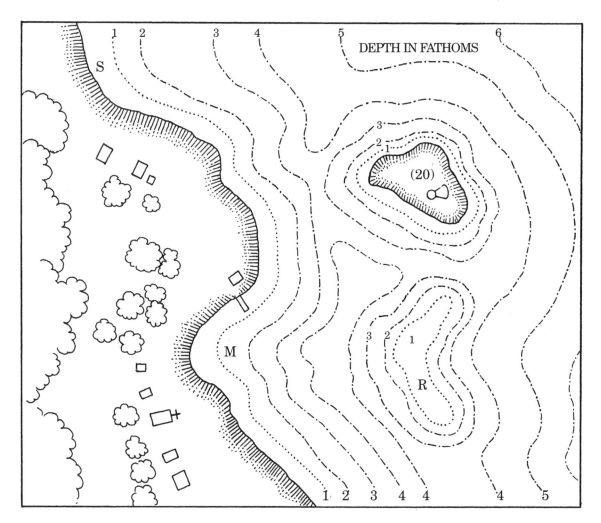

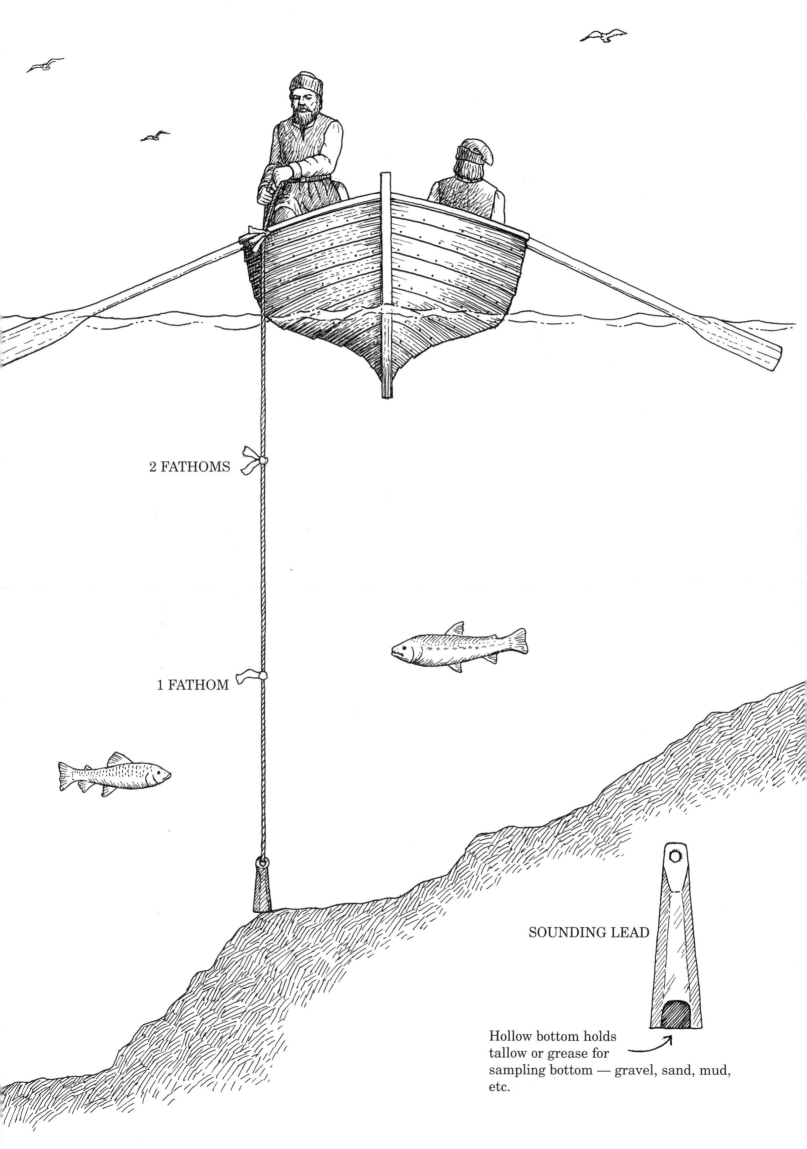

2 FATHOMS

1 FATHOM

SOUNDING LEAD

Hollow bottom holds
tallow or grease for
sampling bottom — gravel, sand, mud,
etc.

MERCATOR'S PROJECTION

The work of Gerhardus Mercator, born in Flanders in 1512, was a great help to deep-sea navigators. Mercator studied philosophy, mathematics and astronomy at the University of Louvain. There he also learned the arts of engraving and instrument making. His first important work was a very detailed map of Flanders. Mercator's work was of such high quality that Emperor Charles V commissioned him to make a *terrestrial* globe which he completed in 1541.

Flanders was becoming a hotbed of religious strife and Mercator, suspected of being a Lutheran, was arrested. Following his release, he moved to Duisburg, a university town on the Rhine. There he became cosmographer to the Duke of Cleves. He also began publishing maps and produced the first modern maps of Europe and Britain.

Mercator soon realized that what the world needed was a really good chart for navigation. Early navigators found it difficult to lay out their courses on a chart because charts made no allowance for the roundness of the earth. The meridians of longitude converge at the poles like the slices of an orange. How could a segment be laid out flat so that a sailor could plot his compass course with a straight line?

Gerardus Mercator found the answer. His solution was to lay out the segments on a flat surface and, treating them as if they were elastic, stretch the tops of the segments until they met. The segments nearest the poles stretched the most. Greenland became huge. The sections between the tropics, where most of the navigation was done, stretched the least. Each segment became a rectangle and was laid out beside the others to form a large world map. Parallel lines of latitude crossed the *meridians* of longitude to form a grid. A navigator could then draw his compass course in a straight line on a flat chart.

In 1569, Mercator published his history-making world map. Today most deep-sea navigation is still done on charts which use the Mercator projection.

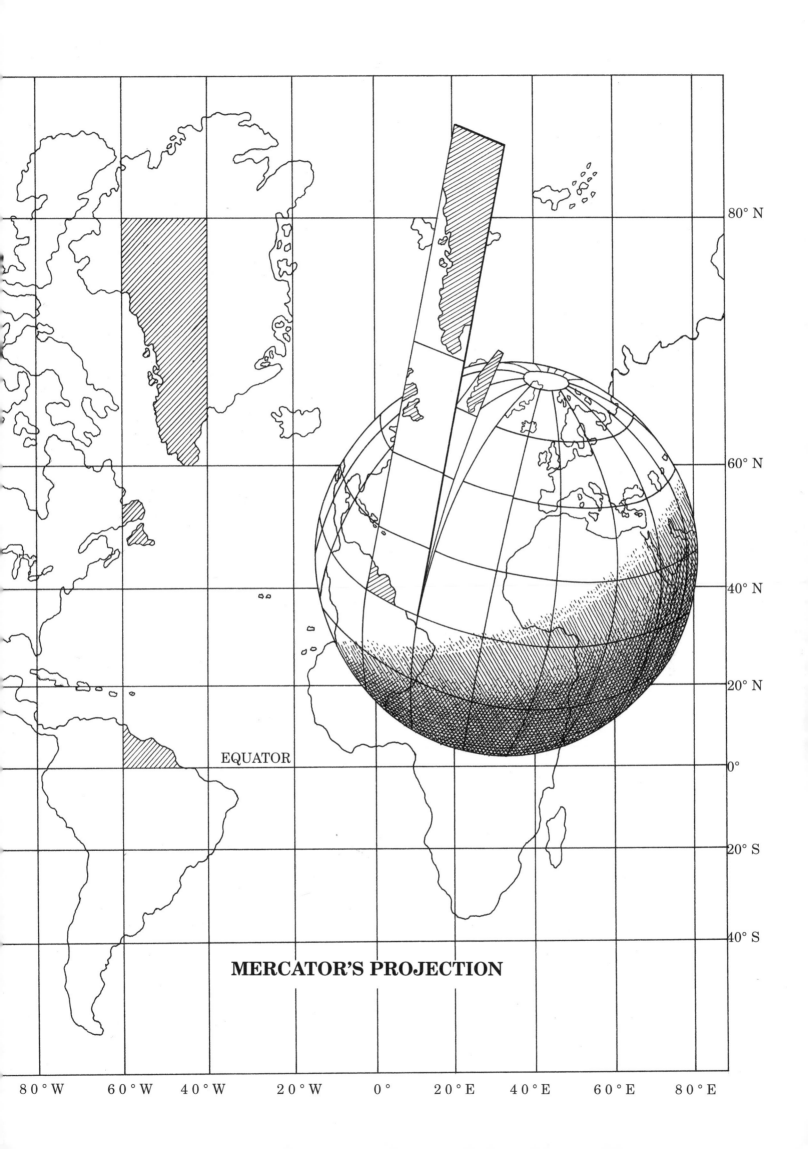

80° N

60° N

40° N

20° N

EQUATOR

0°

20° S

40° S

MERCATOR'S PROJECTION

80°W   60°W   40°W   20°W   0°   20°E   40°E   60°E   80°E

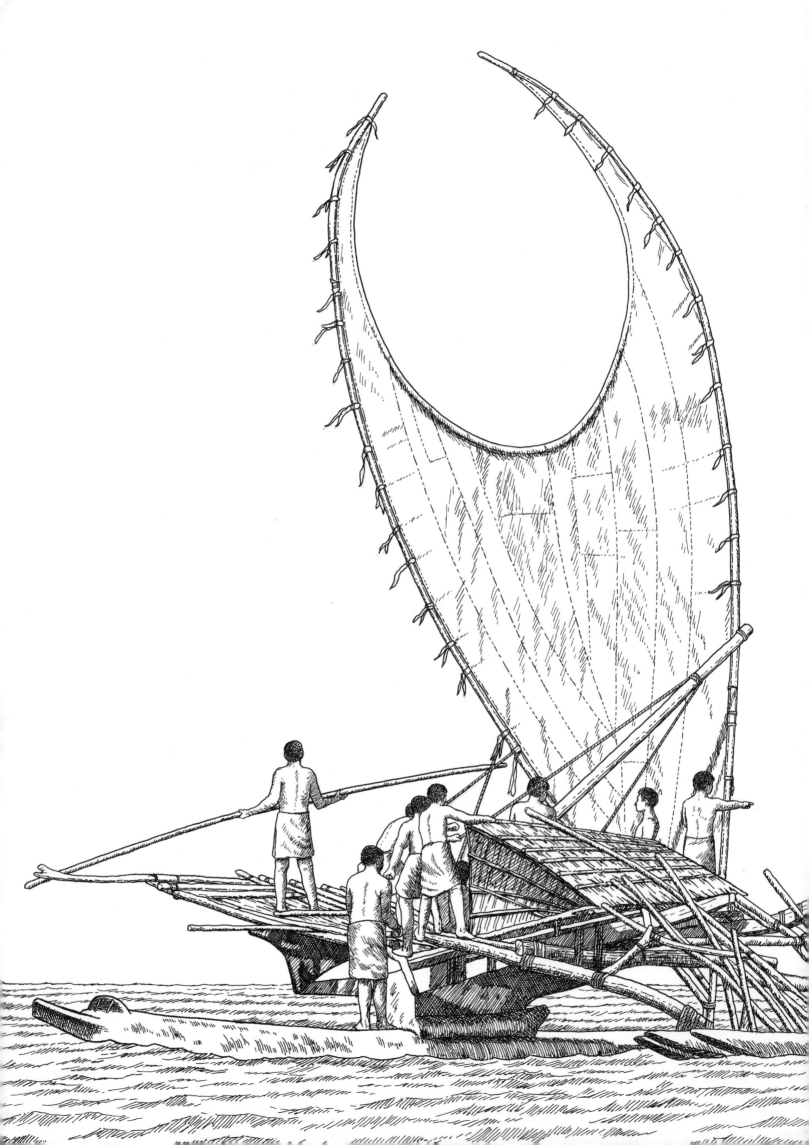

THE PACIFIC NAVIGATORS

When Captain James Cook and other European explorers first encountered the Polynesian Islands, they were surprised to learn that they were already inhabited.

How did these small islands in the middle of the vast Pacific Ocean, thousands of miles from Asia or the Americas, come to be populated? Today, scientists believe the ancestors of the Polynesians migrated from southwest Asia, by way of Indonesia and Melanesia. This migration began over 4,000 years ago. In the course of these moves, the Pacific Islanders developed excellent skills as ship builders.

The ships of the Polynesians evolved from a tradition of dugout canoes carved from a single log. In time they discovered that by attaching outriggers to a single hull or putting two hulls together they could increase both stability and carrying capacity. These vessels called catamarans are considered among the fastest and most seaworthy sailing ships ever designed. Over the centuries they sailed these frail looking but sturdy vessels across the Pacific from Tonga, to Samoa, the Marquesas and finally Hawaii.

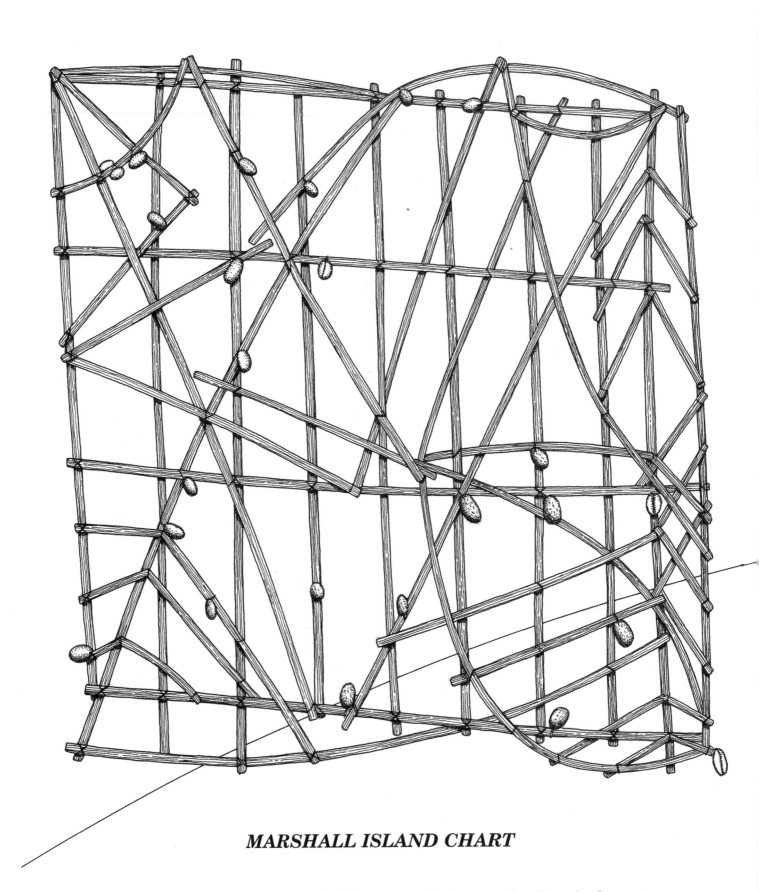

MARSHALL ISLAND CHART

Polynesian navigators were held in very high regard. They had great knowledge of ocean currents, winds, and bird migrations. They knew the position of over 150 stars, and which islands lay under them at different times of the year. The navigators recorded the position of major ocean

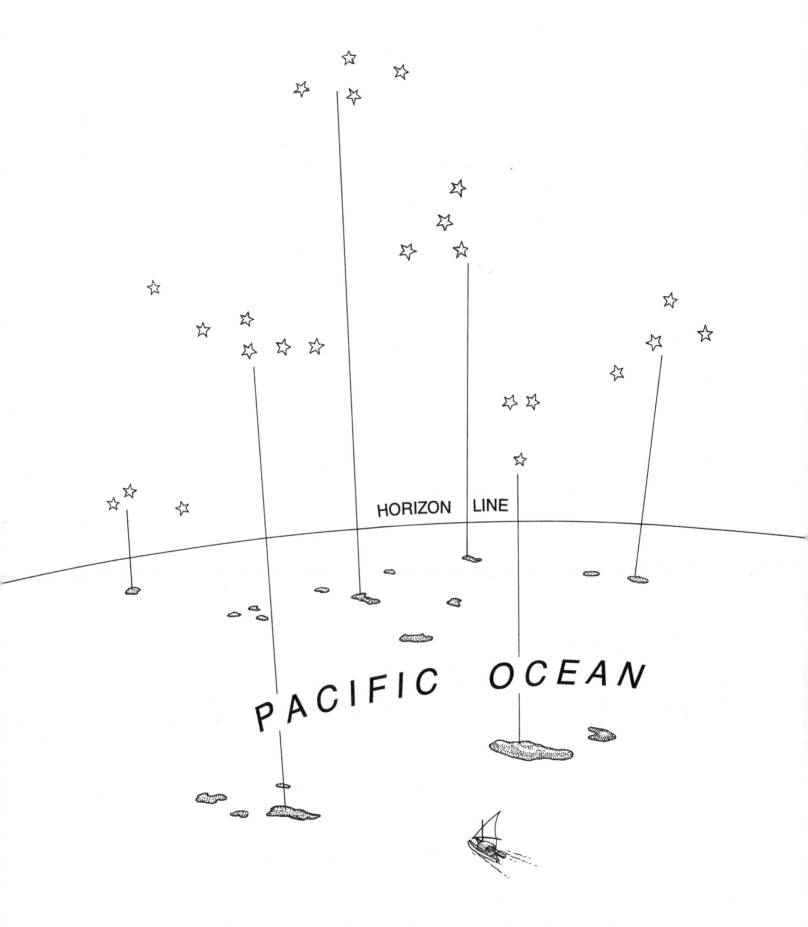

HORIZON LINE

PACIFIC OCEAN

currents on a chart-like network of small sticks tied together. Shells were
tied to this grid to indicate the position of islands. These woven charts
were not taken to sea but were memorized by the navigators. In this way,
knowledge was accumulated and passed on to the next generation.

THE PRINTING OF MAPS

Mapmaking and navigation took a great leap forward with the invention of the *printing press* at Mainz, Germany in the 1440's by Johann Gutenberg.

Prior to Gutenberg, each copy of a book or map had to be handwritten by scribes. These were usually monks working in monastery "scriptoria". Their task was long and tiresome, and often resulted in errors. Each time a map was copied, mistakes invariably crept into the work. If copies were made from copies, a map soon became useless.

The first map printed in Europe came from a German press in 1472. It was a woodcut of a simple, medieval T-O map in an edition of Isidore of Seville's *Etymologies*. Five years later, the first printed edition of Ptolemy's *Geographia*, with its twenty-six plates was produced in Bologna.

The earliest maps were bound into books. But by the second half of the sixteenth century, maps were being printed on separate sheets for pilgrims and other travellers. The best of these were made in Italy. They were printed from engraved copper plates, which produced greater detail than woodblocks.

The first separately printed nautical chart came from Venice in 1539. It was printed by Andrea di Vavassore. Venice became a centre of mapmaking. Many of the first topographical maps of Italy were produced there.

In the sixteenth century, the German states of the north surpassed Italy as makers of fine maps. The Baltic cities of Hamburg, Lübeck and Bremen were prosperous centres of trade. The wealthy merchants there were interested in maps of the countries they traded with. The university towns of Nüremberg, Strasbourg and Basel were full of mathematicians, astronomers and geographers. Nüremberg became known for the quality of its maps, globes and astronomical tables.

EARLY GLOBES

In 1492, the same year that Christopher Columbus sailed across the Atlantic, Martin Behaim in Nüremberg finished his twenty-inch terrestrial globe. His globe was based on Ptolemy. That's why he depicted Asia extending much further to the east than it does, and the Atlantic as much narrower than it is.

The earliest globes were made by printing slices, or gores, of the globe on paper. The gores were then cut out and glued to wooden spheres.

The best known of the German globe makers was Johannes Schöner, a Nüremberg scholar. Two of his globes from the early sixteenth century still exist.

The gores illustrated below are from a globe from around 1540 made by Georg Hartmann.

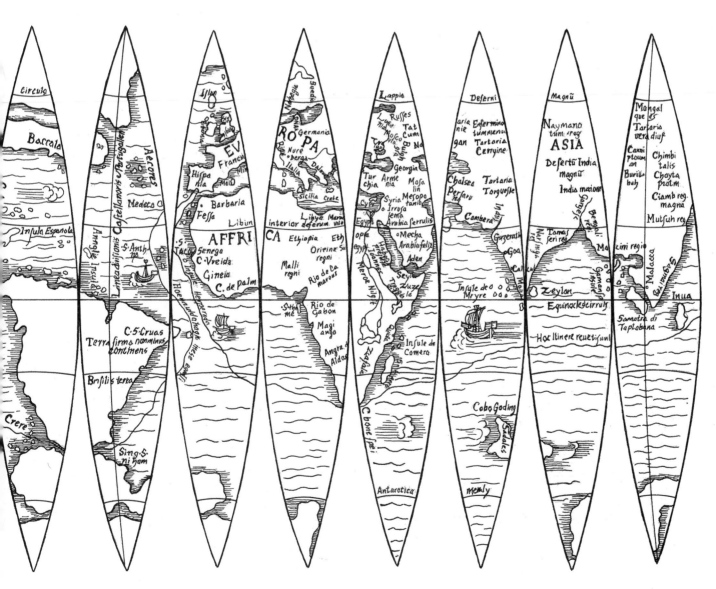

ATLASES

Abraham Ortelius was born in 1527 in Antwerp and lived most of his life there. Ortelius was trained as a map illuminator but soon began buying and selling maps.

One of his best customers was a merchant named Aegidius Hooftmann. Hooftmann used maps to find the fastest routes to move his goods. His office was strewn with maps of all sizes and descriptions. Hooftmann complained about this to Ortelius.

Ortelius solved the problem by gathering together as many reliable single-sheet maps of Europe as possible. He then bound them in one volume. The book he created for Hooftman contained about thirty maps.

After talking to engravers and other mapmakers, Ortelius decided there might be a market for such books of maps. The research, engraving and printing of Ortelius' book of maps took ten years. The *Theatrum Orbis Terrarum* (Theatre of the World) was published in 1570. It contained thirty-five pages of text and fifty-three copperplate maps. It also contained a bibliography of cartographers whose works had been consulted. The *Theatrum* was a great success. By the time of Ortelius' death in 1598, twenty-eight editions had been printed.

Although collections of maps had been printed before, they had never been called "atlases". Atlas, the mythological character who carries the world on his shoulders, first appeared in a collection of maps in 1575. In this book, published by Antonio Lafrevi in Rome, Atlas appeared on the title page. After that, "atlas" became the common word used to describe all books of maps.

WILLEM BLAEU

Toward the end of the sixteenth century, the Netherlands was becoming a sea power, and Amsterdam a centre for world trade and exploration. Under the enlightened government of the Dutch Republic, the arts and sciences flourished.

It was in this setting that the young mapmaker Willem Janzook Blaeu opened his shop in 1596. Blaeu made instruments as well as maps. He had studied for two years with the famous astronomer, Tycho Brahe, and throughout his life maintained an interest in astronomy.

The map trade in Amsterdam was very competitive. Each mapmaker took information from the others' maps. Each tried to be the first to have access to new sources of information. Ships' captains and navigators were carefully questioned and their notes poured over. Blaeu as well as other mapmakers often destroyed their working copies of maps so no one else could see them.

Blaeu, being a good businessman, knew his market. Maps and atlases were becoming status symbols among the wealthy merchant classes. For them, he made beautiful, colorful maps ornamented with gold leaf. Most of these were drawn without parallels or meridians.

The other customers for Blaeu's maps were the Dutch government and seamen. They required accurate, practical maps and sea charts.

Blaeu held the title Map Maker to the Republic. In 1633, he was made head of the hydrography department of the powerful Dutch East India Company. This gave him access to all the geographical and navigational data gathered by the pilots and captains who sailed to India.

Willem Blaeu's first atlas was published in two volumes in 1631. As his business developed, Blaeu had hired the best engravers and printers he could find. He was constantly improving his facilities and making improvements. Following his death in 1637, Blaeu's sons John and Cornelius continued in this tradition.

By 1662, the Blaeu atlas had grown from the original two volumes to twelve volumes with over 600 maps. The Blaeu *Atlas Major*, as it is known, is considered by many experts to be the most beautiful collection of maps ever published.

THE FRENCH ROYAL ACADEMY AND THE SCIENCE OF LONGITUDE

In the time of King Louis XIV (1638-1715) of France, scientists began to investigate the problem of longitude.

Longitude is determined very differently from latitude. For longitude, you need to know exactly when local noon time is at a given location relative to noon at a prime meridian. This information and a sighting of the sun allows navigators to figure out exactly how far they are east or west of the prime meridian.

When Louis came to the throne he was a young man, ambitious and full of confidence. He loved splendour and power and wanted the absolute best of everything. He wanted the most powerful army, the finest art and the grandest architecture. He also wanted the most advanced science.

In 1666, Jean Colbert, Louis' Minister of Finance, established the Royal Academy of Science. As a senior government minister, he had noticed the deplorable lack of accurate maps. He wanted maps that were properly surveyed. He wanted topographic maps. He knew the Royal Academy could do the job.

In 1669, Giovanni Domenico Cassini, an astronomer from Bologna, was made the first director of the Academy. His special interest was the moons of the planet Jupiter, and he published a set of timetables based on their movement. Galileo had discovered the moons and had proposed that since they could be seen from all over the world at once, their movement could be used to help determine longitude, or east-west position.

Cassini wanted to test this hypothesis. First, he devised a method of determining the precise time on the prime meridian when it was noon in some faraway place. He did this by charting the moons of Jupiter, and setting a pendulum clock by the time of their sightings.

The second problem was the accurate measurement of the earth's circumference so that mapmakers would know how much value to assign each of the 360 degrees.

Jean Picard, an astronomer and mathematician with the Royal Academy, was assigned the task of making an arc of the meridian so that a true circumference of the earth could be determined. This prime meridian was established on a line running north and south of Paris.

MEASURING LONGITUDE

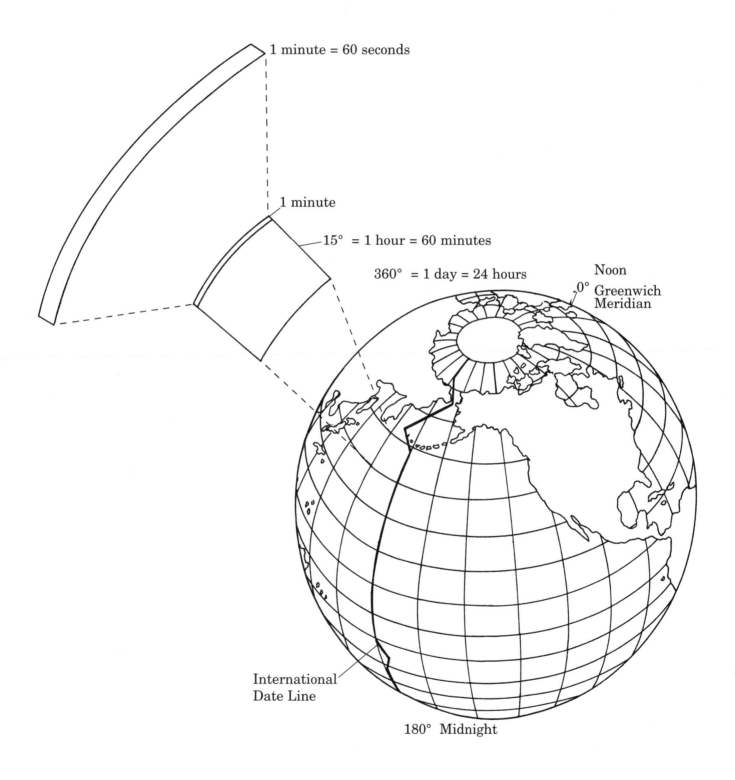

1 minute = 60 seconds

1 minute

15° = 1 hour = 60 minutes

360° = 1 day = 24 hours

Noon

0° Greenwich
Meridian

International
Date Line

180° Midnight

Longitude was very helpful to all kinds of mapmakers, not just navigators. Teams of surveyors with precise instruments and tables of the movement of the moons of Jupiter, now began systematically working their way across France. By careful astronomical observation and *triangulation surveys*, an accurate map of France began to emerge. Some provinces were bigger than had been supposed, others smaller.

When Cassini invited King Louis to view the new map, the king remarked, "Your work has cost me a large part of my state." But Louis liked the job the Royal Academy was doing and his support continued.

Cassini's son Jacques and grandson César Francois continued his work after his death in 1712. Survey teams were sent all over Europe and eventually on expeditions around the world.

In 1783, César Francois Cassini wrote a letter to the English government proposing that England and France join in a triangulation survey across the English Channel. This was the beginning of international cooperation in cartography.

HARRISON'S CHRONOMETER

In the early eighteenth century, determining longitude while at sea was still a major problem. This was because pendulum clocks were quite accurate on solid ground, but unreliable at sea. Many ships were lost becasue of poor navigation.

The British Admiralty decided something must be done about this. In 1713, Parliament offered a prize of 20,000 pounds sterling to anyone who could build an accurate clock that could be carried to sea.

John Harrison, an English carpenter and inventor, took up the challenge. After seven years hard work, he succeeded in building his chronometer. In 1735, it was taken to sea for trials and was found to be very accurate. John Harrison won the prize.

Harrison's chronometer and the refining of the sextant by John Hadley in the 1730's meant that maps and charts became much more accurate. Navigation at sea was vastly improved.

JEAN PICARD'S TELESCOPIC QUADRANT OF 1669

PERAMBULATOR

For measuring distances
over roads

SURVEYOR'S CHAIN

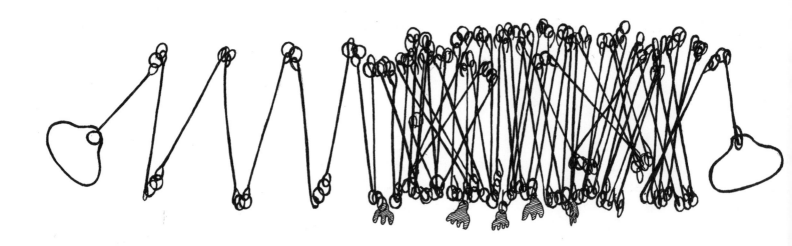

MAPPING THE NATIONS: ENGLAND

Many of the greatest projects of science and engineering have been undertaken for military purposes. The modern mapping of England was begun in the late 1740's following the Scottish rebellion of 1745.

In order to subdue rebel clans and govern the rugged highlands of Scotland, an accurate map was needed. William Roy of the Corps of Engineers was assigned the job. Later, as Director of the Royal Engineers, General Roy arranged for the mapping of England.

The proposal from Cassini about mapping the Channel arrived in England in 1783. Sir Joseph Banks of the Royal Society asked General Roy and the Corps of Engineers to make the survey from London to Dover.

Special rods made of glass were used to measure a base line to begin the survey. Glass was used because, unlike wood or metal, it expands and contracts very little with changes in temperature.

In 1784, a base line of 27,404.0137 feet (about five miles) was measured across Hounslow Heath near London. This was probably the most accurate line that had ever been measured.

The great project of accurately mapping England and France had been proceeding for several years. But the task of connecting the grids across the English Channel was quite another matter.

The job was to be done at night. A series of great triangles would be measured between beacons set up on the English and French coasts.

A very accurate instrument was needed to take the measurements. The Royal Society commissioned Jesse Ramsden to design and build the instrument. Ramsden's theodolite consisted of a moveable brass ring mounted with graduated adjustments, telescopes and small lanterns for night work. It took three years to build.

In the summer of 1787, using Ramsden's theodolite, the job of mapping the Channel was completed.

The triangulation across the Channel revealed considerable errors in the maps of both England and France. General Roy continued to prod the government about making a general survey of Britain. But it was not until after his death that the project really got underway.

The cross-channel survey was a combined effort of the English Royal Society and the Corps of Engineers. But the survey of Britain became a military project and was placed under the Board of Ordnance.

Artillery officers from the Royal Military Academy at Woolwich were considered the most qualified to do the work. They were given special training in drafting and mathematics. The excellent series of travel maps and hiking guides used by Britons and tourists today are known as Ordnance Survey Maps .

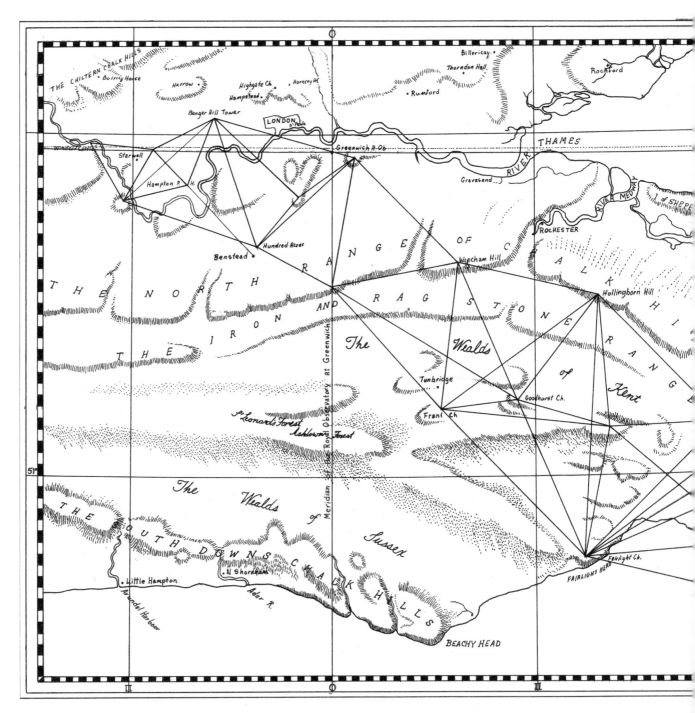

RAMSDEN'S THEODOLITE

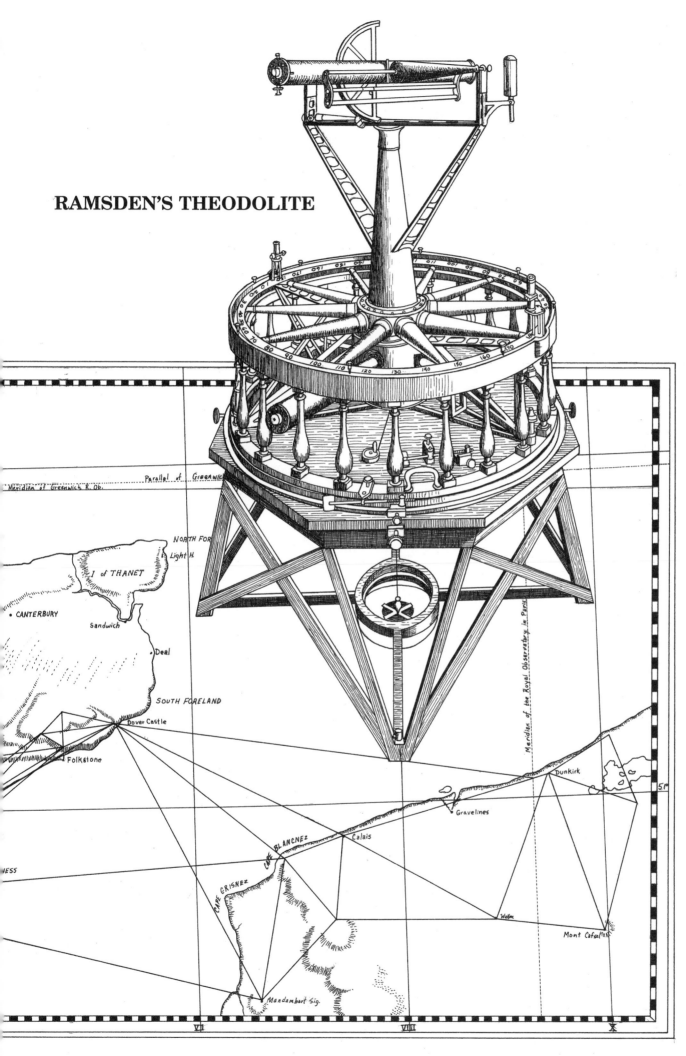

MAPPING THE NATIONS: NORTH AMERICA

Most of Europe had been mapped by the end of the eighteenth century with some degree of accuracy. But the mapping of the American continents had only just begun.

The treaties that ended the American Revolution defined territory in vague terms. No boundaries had been surveyed nor markers placed. When the United States purchased the Louisiana Territory from France in 1803, it doubled the size of U.S. territory. But what had really been bought? The purchase included the Rocky Mountains — about which hardly anything was known.

Samuel Hearne, a British explorer in Western Canada, had first established the idea of a Continental Divide. The height and extent of this great ridge, now known as the Rocky Mountains, could only be imagined.

On a map of 1795 by the British cartographer Aaron Arrowsmith, the elevation of the Rockies was thought to be about 3,500 feet — less than a quarter of their real height!

This was the great unknown territory into which the explorers and mapmakers of the west were sent.

In May, 1804, Meriwether Lewis and William Clark set out from St. Louis with a party of forty-five to explore the Louisiana Purchase. They travelled by keelboat up the Missouri River into the Dakotas. During the winter of 1804–05, they stayed in the villages of the Mandan people. From them, they learned much about the territory to the west. The Indians drew charts on the ground with sticks, or with charcoal on skins. William Clark carefully copied these into his notebooks. They proved to be very reliable.

In the spring, Lewis and Clark continued westward through Montana and Idaho. There they discovered the Snake and Columbia Rivers. In late 1805, the explorers reached the Pacific Coast.

Lewis and Clark returned to St. Louis in the fall of 1806. The map based on the explorers' notes was published in 1814. Although it was not a scientific work compared to that of European mapmakers, it did lay out a framework for those who followed.

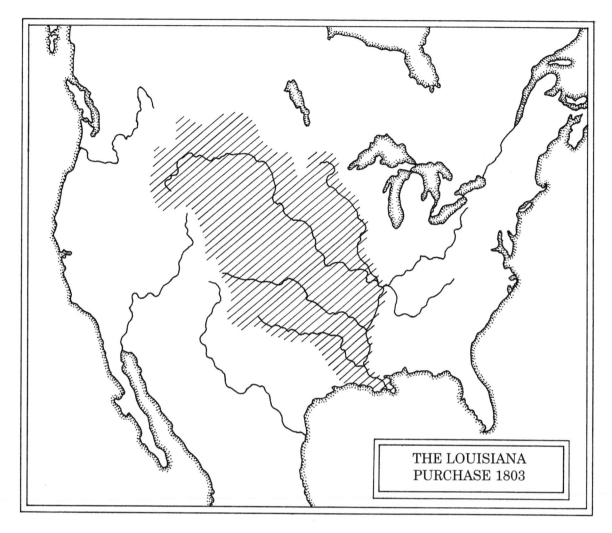

THE LOUISIANA
PURCHASE 1803

In 1838, the Corps of Topographical Engineers took over the task of *surveying* and mapping the American West. Among the most famous of this small elite group was John C. Fremont. He spent two years with French scientist Joseph Nicollet exploring and mapping Minnesota and the Dakotas. Nicollet introduced Fremont to the scientific technique of using a *barometer* to obtain one's altitude, or height, above sea level.

In 1842, Fremont set out from St. Louis on his own expedition to explore and map the west beyond the Mississippi. With him travelled Charles Preuss. Preuss was a German-born and trained surveyor and mapmaker who preferred the drafting board to horseback. No wonder Fremont led the expedition while Preuss sketched the terrain!

Over the next ten years, Fremont and Preuss mapped much of the territory of Oregon, Washington, Utah, Nevada and California. Perhaps most importantly, they mapped the Oregon Trail. This was a path through the Rocky Mountains, and it paved the way for wagon trains of settlers from the east.

PUTTING IT ALL TOGETHER

By the last quarter of the nineteenth century, most European countries were making good topographical maps. The International Hydrographic Survey was established to map the coast and harbours of the world. This organization was led by Britain, France and the Netherlands, with its headquarters in Monaco.

Mapmaking was becoming an international concern but there were still problems. No common standards or scales existed. And — perhaps the biggest problem of all — there was no common prime meridian. Each country had its own!

At the third International Congress of Geographers held in Vienna in 1881, the members discussed establishing Greenwich, England as the Prime Meridian. They thought the line running through the Bering Strait between Siberia and Alaska should be the *International Date Line*. In 1884, the first International Meridian Conference held in Washington adopted Greenwich as the Prime Meridian. It also adopted *International Standard Time*.

At following conferences, other joint projects were discussed, including a world map. Further international efforts were interrupted by World War I and not begun again until after World War II.

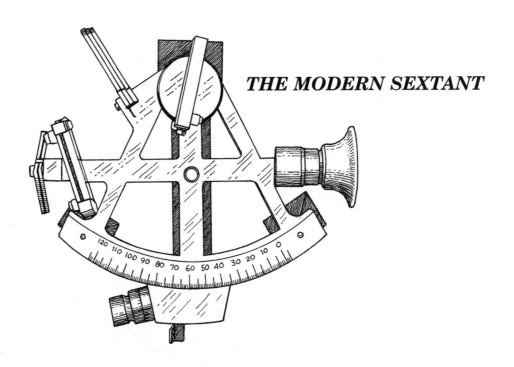

THE MODERN SEXTANT

THE PRIME MERIDIAN, GREENWICH

THE LAST PLACES ON EARTH

The last places on earth to be explored, mapped and charted were the north and south polar regions.

Since discovering North and South America, the European explorers had been trying to find passages around or through them. These efforts led them to the north and south extremes of the continents — to the Poles.

For centuries, explorers whose names are now famous — Martin Frobisher, John Davis, Henry Hudson, William Baffin, William Parry and Sir John Franklin — had searched for the elusive Northwest Passage from the Atlantic to the Pacific. Many, like Hudson and Franklin, died in the attempt. Although they did not find the Passage, each explorer added to our knowledge of what was at the top of the globe.

Other European explorers had been looking for a way to reach the Far East over the top of Asia — a Northeast Passage. Willem Barents, Vitus Bering and Dimitri Laptev attempted to penetrate the ice-packed seas north of Siberia. In doing so, they defined much of the Arctic coast of Asia.

In 1878, an expedition led by the Swedish explorer Nils Nordenskjöld left Tromsö, Norway in the steam bark Vega. In July of 1879, after having spent the winter frozen in the Arctic ice, the Vega emerged through the open waters of the Bering Strait. The Northeast Passage had been found!

The nature of the north polar region itself was still a mystery. The Norwegian scientist and explorer Fritdjof Nansen believed the ice cap was not a land mass but a great frozen sea. In 1893 he allowed his polar ship *Fram* to be locked into the ice and drift across the top of the world. In 1895 he and Frederik Johansen set off on skis toward the pole. They came within 300 km. of reaching it — 86° 13' the "farthest north" yet achieved.

In 1906 another Norwegian, Roald Amundsen, on an expedition to study the north magnetic pole, successfully navigated the Northwest Passage from Lancaster Sound to Alaska. It had taken 400 years and the loss of many lives — but the Passage had been discovered at last.

GREENLAND DRIFTWOOD MAPS

For several thousand years, native people navigated their skin-covered kayaks along the rugged coasts of Greenland. To help them find their way back to their settlements, they carved notches in pieces of driftwood. Each notch represented an indentation in the coast line made by a bay or fjord. In this way, the kayaker could keep track of how many bays he was from home.

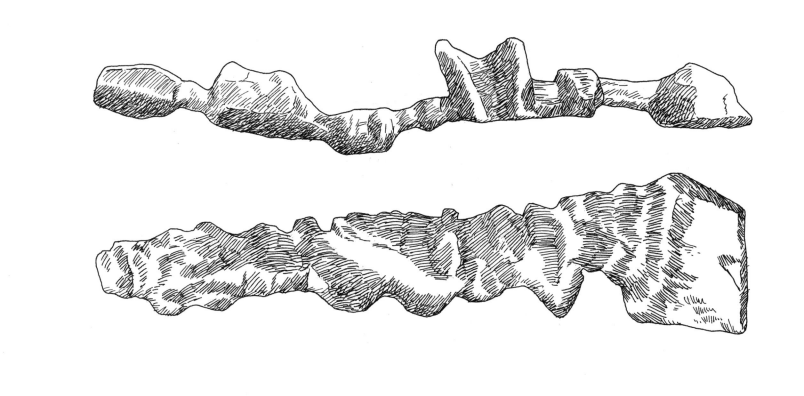

SCIENTIFIC TECHNIQUES FOR MAPPING

For modern cartographers, the two greatest inventions would have to be photography and aircraft.

Photography was invented in the mid-nineteenth century. Its potential usefulness to topographical surveyors was quickly realized.

At first, photographs taken from tall buildings and towers were used in mapping, especially of urban areas. But soon photographers were trying to suspend cameras from kites and taking them up in hot air balloons.

Aimé Laussedat, a French army officer, was a pioneer in the field of *photogrammetry*. In 1859, Laussedat developed a special camera that was combined with a theodolite for mapping. He photographed the same object from several points of view in order to "fix" its position. After a number of objects had been fixed, the area between could be filled in with some degree of accuracy.

In 1906, Theodor Scheimpflug, an Austrian, designed a camera for aerial photogrammetry. It had eight lenses — one vertical, and seven arranged in a circle around it at angles. Eight photographs were taken at the same time for a complete *panoramic* view.

However, in 1906, this camera was not all that useful. Aircraft were still in their earliest stages of development, and the hot air balloon was very unstable. Because of all the joggling around, it was almost impossible for photographers to get good pictures from up in the air.

After World War I, many small businessmen bought surplus war planes, and installed cameras in them. They hired themselves and their equipment out to governments, engineering firms and resource developers. Soon the government mapping agencies began using aerial photogrammetric techniques on a regular basis. Once the photographs had been taken, there was still much work to be done on the ground. The overlapping images had to be projected and plotted mechanically.

Today, cartographers use still more sophisticated technology. The first great breakthroughs came with the use of radar and sonar. In war time, these radio signals helped detect enemy aircraft and submarines. Today, they are used by mapmakers to penetrate clouds and dense forests, and to survey the bottom of the deepest seas.

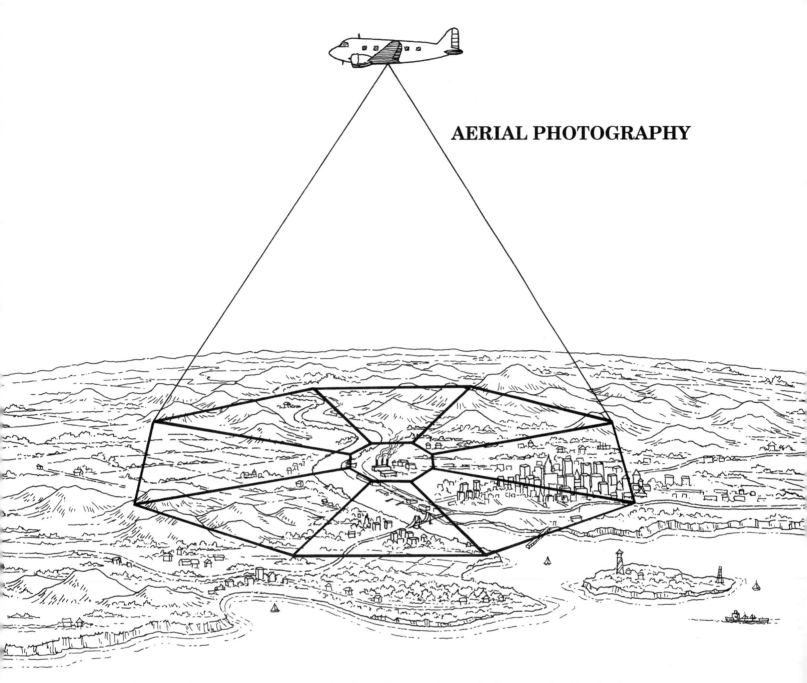

Geographers are concerned with the surface of the earth. *Geologists* are interested in what lies below it. This kind of work requires special equipment. The *magnetometer* is used to detect subtle differences in the earth's magnetism. For instance, various rock formations and ore deposits have different magnetic levels. The results are plotted as lines on rolls of paper.

Seismographs, similar to those used to detect earthquakes, measure seismic waves reflected by rocks from small explosions at the surface. The waves from the sound penetrate various types of rock formations differently. The differences are recorded as lines. The lines reveal variations in the structure below the surface of the earth.

Before computers, map production — from the initial survey to the printed product — could take years. Now, satellite surveys and computer printouts have shortened the process to a matter of hours or minutes.

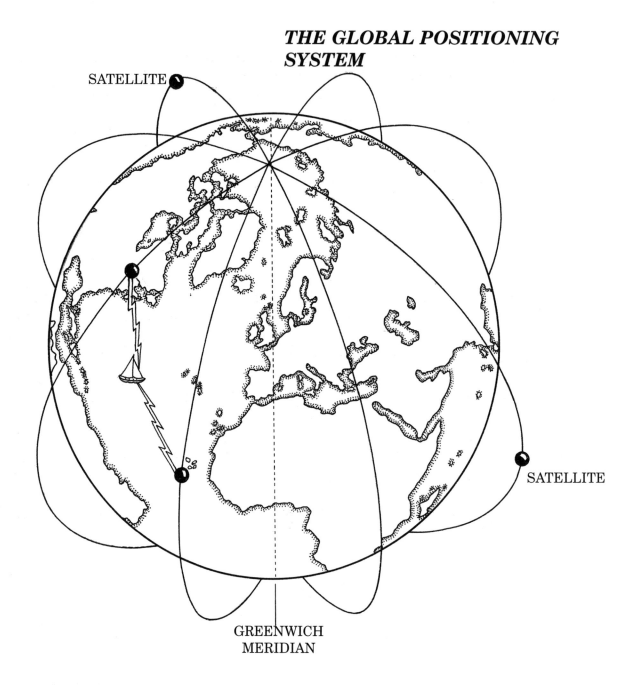

THE GLOBAL POSITIONING SYSTEM

SATELLITE

SATELLITE

GREENWICH
MERIDIAN

MODERN NAVIGATION SYSTEMS

An increasingly mobile population has brought the development of modern transportation systems. At any one time there are thousands of modern aircraft moving through the air around the world. Huge freighters and oil tankers ply the sea lanes carrying precious and potentially hazardous cargoes. These crowded corridors can only be managed with the most accurate and reliable navigation systems.

Modern navigation aids for ships and airplanes employ all the latest scientific technology.

Radar systems enable pilots to monitor the position of other aircraft near them. These systems can also detect cloud cover and storms. On the ground, radar is used by air traffic controllers to assign "airspace" and control the landing and take-off of aircraft.

Automatic pilots on airplanes and ships mean that courses can be set and maintained with *gyrocompasses* and radio signals. The slightest deviations in course or speed are adjusted automatically. Pilots can relax — at least a little!

The LORAN (Long Range Aids to Navigation) system was begun in the late 1950's. By the mid 1970's, most of the world was covered by a network of LORAN stations transmitting pulsed radio signals. These multiple signals received by ships and aircraft give them a very accurate fix on their position.

Perhaps the most amazing development in navigation is the GPS (Global Positioning System). GPS measures radio signals based on the Doppler shift phenomenon. In other words, it measures variations in the frequency of radio waves between the source of the signal (the satellite) and the receiving station (a ship). The system consists of multiple satellites, ground tracking stations, computing facilities, an injection station, time signals and the receiver and computer.

When the GPS was first developed in the mid 1960's, it was very expensive. It was also top secret and available only for military purposes. In the late 1960's, the system became available for civilian use.

GPS RECEIVER AND DISPLAY

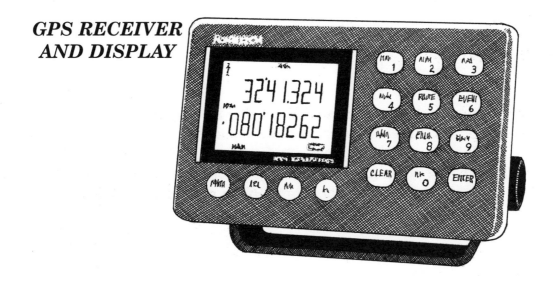

Today, advances in technology and the smaller size of computers and receivers have made the GPS available to yachtsmen — and even hikers. A sailor at the helm of his small ship can press a button on a hand-held receiver and find his exact longitude and latitude within a few meters anywhere in the world!

This technology is truly amazing. But, if the battery dies and electronic systems fail, our sailor, like his distant ancestors, can turn his eyes once again to the sky.

GLOSSARY

ALMANAC. A book that gives facts about the weather, the tides, and the rising and setting of the sun for each day of the year.

ARCHAEOLOGIST. A person who studies ancient times and peoples through the things that they have made or built.

ASTRONOMER. A person who studies the sun, planets, moon, and stars.

AUTOMATIC PILOT. A device or system that steers and guides a ship or aircraft by itself.

BAROMETER. An instrument for measuring air pressure. A barometer can be used to forecast changes in the weather, and to find the height above sea level.

CARTOGRAPHY. The making of maps or charts.

CIRCUMFERENCE. The distance around the outside of a circle.

COMPASS. An instrument for showing directions, with a moving needle that always points North.

COSMOLOGY. The science dealing with the study of the universe as a whole.

EQUINOX. A time of year in spring and autumn when the day and night are of equal length all over the world. The equinoxes happen about March 21 and September 23.

GEOLOGIST. A person who studies rocks, mountains, and cliffs to learn more about the earth and its history.

GYROCOMPASS. An instrument for determining direction, using the rotation motion of the earth and a spinning gyroscope.

HABITABLE. Places capable of supporting life.

HYDROGRAPHY. The study and mapping of the surface of the earth's waters, such as seas, lakes, and rivers.

INTERNATIONAL DATE LINE. An invented line opposite the Greenwich Meridian on the earth at or near 180 degrees longitude when the date changes by one day when the line is crossed.

INTERNATIONAL STANDARD TIME. The official time for any of the twenty-four time zones in which the world is divided.

LATITUDE. The distance measured in degrees on the earth's surface north or south of the equator.

LONGITUDE. The distance measured in degrees on the earth's surface east or west of a line on the map passing through Greenwich, England to the North and South Poles.

MAGNETIC NORTH. The direction toward which the needle of a compass points. In most cases, it is not True North.

MAGNETOMETER. An instrument that detects subtle differences in the earth's magnetism.

MERIDIAN. Any line of longitude.

NAVIGATION. The science of working out the correct route for a ship or aircraft.

PANORAMIC. Wide, complete, all-around.

PHOTOGRAMMETRY. Map-making from photographs.

PRECESSION OF THE EQUINOXES. The gradual westward movement of the two points on the equator where the sun crosses it on the dates of the equinox.

PRIME MERIDIAN. The line that runs vertically from the North to South Poles through the Greenwich Observatory in England, from which longitude is measured.

PRINTING PRESS. A machine that prints words and pictures by pressing an inked image on paper.

SEISMOGRAPH. An instrument that measures the strength of earthquakes and how long they last.

SOUNDING. Measuring the depth of water.

SURVEYING. Measuring and mapping the size, shape, boundaries, etc. of parts of the earth's surface.

TERRESTRIAL. Of the earth.

THEODOLITE. A surveying instrument used for measuring angles.

TOPOGRAPHY. The surface features of a region, such as hills, rivers, roads, etc.

TRIANGULATION SURVEY. Measuring and mapping a region by dividing it into triangles.